An Uncommon Vocabulary
(4th Edition Revised)

An Uncommon Vocabulary
(4th Edition Revised)

J im B oyd

An Uncommon Vocabulary

Fourth Edition, Revised

Copyright © 2012, 2014, 2015, 2017 by Jim Boyd

ISBN: 9780985643577 (Print Fourth Edition, Revised)
ISBN: 0985643579

Printed in the United States of America

Preface

There are two activities in life that are essential to one's happiness. The first is to have one's day (to explore, engage and enjoy life), and the second is to say one's say (to say the words to oneself and to others that one needs to say).

"An Uncommon Vocabulary" is an A to Z book of common and uncommon words and phrases that are described in ways better suited to them in the opinion of the author.

The concepts describe herein are working definitions, definitions that can be brought to mind to facilitate one's thinking and actions within a given set of circumstances.

When a working definition is properly occasioned (brought to mind at the appropriate time and in the appropriate circumstances), advantageous effects flow from it.

In this way, one's personal narratives (descriptions and prescriptions) are made richer and more rewarding, and one becomes more coherent and positive in dealing with everyday events.

—JB

Prologue

Men are four:

He who knows not and knows not that he knows not: he is a fool – shun him.

He who knows not and knows that he knows not: he is simple – teach him.

He who knows and knows not that he knows: he is asleep – wake him.

He who knows and knows that he knows: he is wise – follow him.

Arab Proverb

Words and Phrases

A

Absolute, Absurdity, Accept, Accomplishment, Acknowledgement, Act One's Age, Action, Adapt, Addicted to Not Being Addicted, Advantage, Affected, Affections, Aftertaste, Afterthought, Age, Agenda, Aggravate an Injury, Aggressively Patient, Agitation, Agnostic, Ambiguity, Ambition, Amusement, Anger, Animosity, Annoyance, Answer, Anticipate, Anxiety, Appearance, Appeaser, Appreciating One's Mortality, Appropriate Request, Arrogance, Arrogant, Ask for Help, Asleep, Asleep at the Wheel, Aspire to be Supernatural, Atheist, Attend, Attitude, Attractiveness, Authority Figure, Aware, Awe

B

Baby Steps, Back Off, Bad Action, Bad Attitude, Bad Bargain, Bad Habit, Bad Memory, Bad Request, Badness, Baggage, Balance, Banish the Thought, Be Different, Beauty, Behave, Behavior,

Being Easy On Oneself, Being Fair with Oneself, Being Hard on Oneself, Being Human, Belief, Belief System, Bend, Best Apology, Best Solution, Best Trick, Better, Big Stuff, Birth, Bitched, Bitterness, Blame Game, Bleeding Heart, Bliss, Bluff, Bogged Down, Boldness, Bond, Bored, Born, Bottom Line, Bravery, Breadcrumb, Break, Break a Bad Habit, Break a Spell, Breakdown, Breakthrough, Breathe, Buy Time

C

Call a Spade a Spade, Call a Timeout, Call Out, Calm Down, Calmness, Captivity, Care for Oneself, Care Less, Caterwaul, Caution, Cautious, Cease and Desist, Center of Gravity, Center Stage, Certain Truth, Certainty, Chain of Events, Challenge, Change, Chaos, Character, Charity, Cheap Vice, Cheese, Childish, Chinks in the Armor, Circumstances, Clarify, Classification, Clean House, Cleaning, Clear Mind, Cleverness, Closed Book, Closed-Mindedness, Clueless, Coast, Coast to the Line, Code of Conduct, Cognitive Dissonance, Coherent, Cold War, Colloquialist, Collywobbles, Comeback, Comeuppance, Compartmental-ization, Compassionate, Competition, Competitor, Complacency, Complain, Complexity, Composure, Comprehend, Compulsion, Con, Con(2), Concentrate, Concern, Conformist, Confusion, Congregation, Consequences, Conservative, Consider, Construct, Contempt, Contentment, Contradictions, Contrarian, Conviction, Convinced, Cooler, Cooperate, Core Belief, Core Beliefs, Courage, Courageous, Coward, Cowardice, Creation, Creativity, Criteria for Belief or Disbelief, Criticism, Crook, Crutch, Cunning, Curiosity, Cynic

D

Dangerous Living, Dangerous Rhetoric, Dangling, Daring, Dark Truth, Darkly Recalcitrant, Dead and Buried, Dead-End, Deadhead, Death, Debacle, Deceiver, Deception, Decide, Decide Not to Decide, Deconstruct, Defeat, Deference, Defiant, Delayed Reactions, Delightful Occupations, Delusion, Demagogue, Demands of the Day, Demerit, Demon, Dent. Dependencies, Dependency, Dependent, Derelict, Desire, Despair, Detach, Deterioration, Die, Differences of Opinion, Difficulty, Diminishment, Dimwit, Direct Question, Dirt, Disadvantage, Disambiguation, Disappointment, Disbelief, Discipline, Discourage, Disengage, Disgusting, Dishonor, Disinterestedness, Dismiss a Thought, Disown, Displaced Aggression, Distillate, Distracted, Do Less, Do More, Do the Deed, Do the Math, Dogma, Don't Know. Don't Care, Done Deal, Doubt, Doubter, Drama, Draw a Line in the Sand, Dream, Dreamer, Driven, Dust, Duty, Dysfunctional Thought

E

Easy Answer, Easy Rider, Easy Street, Easy Way, Edges of a Problem, Educate Oneself, Effective, Efficient, Effort, Elephant in the Room, Elevate One's Game, Emotional Intelligence, Emotional Sobriety, Emotive State, Empathy, Empower Oneself, Emptiness, Encourage, End of Day, Endeavor, Enduring Sentiment, Enemy, Engage Life, Enjoy Life, Enjoy the Scenery, Enlightenment, Enough is Enough, Entertainment, Enthusiasm, Envious, Escapism, Essence, Etching, Event, Ever-Growing Calm, Evidence, Evil, Evolution, Exaggerate, Excitement, Excuse, Exercise in Futility, Exhaustion, Exist, Exonerate, Exorcise, Experience, Experiment, Explicit Thought, Explicit You, Explore, Externally Validate, Extremism, Eyes Wide Open

F

Facilitate, Fact, Fail Forward, Failed Experiment, Failure, Fair Price, Faith, Faithful, Fall Off the Wagon, False Prophet, Fanciful Notion, Far Side, Faster, Fate, Fathom, Fatigue, Fear, Fear Monger, Fearless Leader, Fed Up, Fight, Final Answer, Find One's Way, Finish, First Good Step in Addressing the Present, First Good Step in Breaking a Harmful Habit, First Good Step in Forgetting the Past, First Good Step in Helping Oneself, First Good Step in Making an Adjustment, First Good Step in Preparing for the Future, First Good Step in Pursuing Happiness, First Principle, Flight, Flinching, Flip Side, Fly by the Seat of One's Pants, Focus, Follow, Follow the Breadcrumbs, Follower, Fool, Foolhardy, Foolish Thrift, Foolishness, Forethought, Forget, Forget Time, Forgive, Forgiveness, Fortunate, Fortune, Frame of Reference, Free, Free Spirit, Free Will, Friend, Friendly Game, Frustration, Fulfillment, Fully Engaged, Fun, Futility, Future, Fuzziness, Fuzzy Rule, Fuzzy Thinking, Fuzzy Universe

G

Gain Insight, Gain Traction, Game, Game Player, General Order of Things, Generalize, Generous, Genuineness, Get, Get a Grip, Get Back in the Saddle, Get One's Blood Up, Get Real, Gift, Give the Benefit of the Doubt, Give Up, Give-Up in the Get, Glutton, Glutton for Punishment, Glutton's Punishment, Go with the Flow, Goal, Going the Extra Mile, Good Action, Good Attitude, Good Bargain,

An Uncommon Vocabulary (4th Edition Revised)

Good Communication, Good Decision, Good Enough, Good Fortune, Good Journey, Good Memory, Good Request, Good Riddance, Goodness, Grace, Graceful, Grasping at Straws, Greedy, Grief, Grieving Process, Grinder, Grounded, Growth Hormone, Guilt, Gullible

H

Habit, Half-Truth, Hangover, Happiness, Happiness and Unhappiness, Harass, Hard Head, Hard Rider, Hard Way, Harm, Harmony, Harshness, Hate, Hateful, Having One's Day, Heal from the Inside Out, Health, Heart of Hearts, Heart of the Problem, Heart of Things, Heaven on Earth, Hell on Earth, Here and Now, Hero, Hero Worship, Hide and Seek, High-Yield Investment, Higher Self, Hindsight, History, Holistic Thought, Honesty, Honor, Hope, Hot Head, Human Being, Humanist, Humanity, Humility, Humor, Hunger, Hunker Down, Hurry, Hype, Hypocrite, Hypothesis

I

Idea, Ideal, Idealism, Idealist, Ideals, Idiocy, Idiot, Ignorance, Illegitimate Suffering, Illusion, Illusion of Control, Imagine, Impactful, Imperfection, Impetus Behind Evolution, Implicit Thought, Implicit You, Impossible, Improve Oneself, Indecision, Independent, Indiscretion, Individualized Accomplishment, Individualized Guilt, Indulge, Ineffectualness, Inertia, Inferior Opponent, Inferiority Complex, Influence, Information, Innovate, Insanity, Inspiration, Instinct, Insubordination, Insult, Integrity, Intellectual, Intelligence, Intelligent, Intention, Intentional Harm, Intolerant, Intrusion, Intuition, Invincible, Irksomeness of Change, Irrationality, Irregularities, Irrelevant

J

Jerk, Joke, Joy, Joyful, Judge, Judge Rightly, Justice

K

Karmic Justice, Keep it Simple, Keep One's Distance, Kid at Heart, Kid Gloves, Kindness, Kindness to the Unkind, Kindred Spirit, Knockdown, Knot, Know, Knowledge, Knowledgeable, Known Universe

L

Language, Last Straw, Lasting Agreement, Laughter, Law of Attraction, Leader, Learn, Leave It and Move On, Legitimate Suffering, Leisure Time, Leniency, Lesser Self, Lesson, Let Bygones Be Bygones, Let Sleeping Dogs Lie, Liberal, Lie, Life, Life(2), Life-Cycle of an Effort, Life's Guarantees, Limit, Listen, Live, Live and Let Live, Live in the Present, Live with Contradictions, Liveliness, Living, Logic, Logical Conclusion, Loser's Attitude, Losing Proposition, Loss Limit, Lost in the Trees, Love, Luck, Lucky

M

Madness, Make a Smooth Transition, Maladjusted, Malarkey, Man's Rightful Dominion over Nature, Manage, Manage Money, Martyr, Masochist, Math, Mature, Maudlin Mind, Meander, Meaning, Meaning-of-Life, Measured Response, Mental Anguish, Merit, Mess Maker, Metamorphosis, Methodical, Mettle, Mind, Minimize, Miracle, Misbehave, Misogynist, Mistake, Mitigate, Mixed Bag, Moderate, Moderation, Mojo, Momentum, Monkey on One's Back, Moral Judgment, Morning Sun, Mortal Wound,

An Uncommon Vocabulary (4th Edition Revised)

Motion, Motivated, Motive, Move On, Muddle Through, Mull Over, Mystery, Mystify

N
Navigate, Near Side, Necessary, Need, Negative, Neurosis, New Day, Niche, Nihilist, No Action, No-Nonsense Person, Noble Pretensions of Ignoble Persons, Nonconformist, Nonsense, Nostalgia, Not-a-Penny, Not-To-Do List, Nothing, Nothingness, Numero Uno

O
Obedience, Obligation, Obsession, Obstructionist, Obvious, Obvious Defense, Off-Balance Opponent, Offense, On the Edge of Chaos, On Time, One's Book, One's Life, One's Path, One's Purpose in Life, One's Worth, One-Sided Relationship, Open Book, Open-Mindedness, Operative Words, Opinionated Unnecessarily, Opportunism, Opportunity Cost, Optimism, Optimist, Optimistic, Option-in-One's Pocket, Order, Orderliness, Organism, Out-Spoken, Overachiever, Overcommit, Overkill, Overreact

P
Pace Oneself, Pain, Panic, Pantheist, Paralysis, Pardon, Passions, Past, Path to Redemption, Patience, Pay the Piper, Peace of Mind, Pencil, Perfection, Perfectionist, Persist, Persistent Dissatisfaction, Personal Narrative, Personal Taboos, Personality, Perspective, Pessimism, Pessimist, Pessimistic, Petted and Pampered, Philosopher, Physician, Pickle, Picky, Pitiful Offense, Pivot, Plan, Plan Less, Planet Earth, Plans, Play, Play Dumb, Play for Fun, Pleasure, Plug In, Point, Poison, Positional Advantage, Positional Disadvantage, Positive, Possessed,

Possible, Pothole, Poverty, Power, Powerful, Practicality, Prepare, Present, Press On, Pressure, Pretension, Price, Price Control, Pride, Primal Fear, Principle, Principled, Proactive, Procedure, Procrastinate, Progress, Progressive, Promise, Proof, Punctual, Purity, Purpose, Pursue Excellence, Pursue Happiness, Push Back, Put Up a Front

Q
Quality Experience, Question, Quiet Interval, Quitter

R
Rabbit Hole, Radical Idea, Radical Thinker, Rash Action, Rational Behavior, React, Readiness, Realist, Reality, Reality-As-It-Is, Really?, Reason, Reasonable, Reasonable Probability, Reassurance, Rebel, Reborn, Recipe for Weight Loss, Reciprocity, Reckless Plan, Reconcile, Recover, Reductionist, Reductionist Process, Reform, Reformer, Refuse to Imagine, Regret, Regularities, Relax, Relevant, Remarkable, Remedy, Remedy Boredom, Remedy Loneliness, Remembrance, Reminder, Remorse, Remorseful, Residue, Resilient, Resolution, Resolve, Respite, Responsibleness, Rest, Result, Resurrect, Return to Sender, Revenge, Reverse Psychology, Revolution, Revolving-Door Universe, Rhetoric, Ridiculousness, Right, Right (2), Right Action, Right Answer, Right Question, Righteousness, Rise and Shine, Rise to the Occasion, Risky Business, Rock Bottom, Rule, Rule Worth Following, Ruminate, Rumor

S
Sadist, Sadness, Safety, Safety Valve, Sag, Sanity, Saying One's Say, Scar, Scheme, Science, Scientific Method, Score, Scratch Where It Itches, Secret to a Long Life, Self, Self Forgive, Self-Acceptance,

An Uncommon Vocabulary (4th Edition Revised)

Self-Assertion, Self-Compassion, Self-Confidence, Self-Control, Self-Deception, Self-Defeating, Self-Defense, Self-Deprivation, Self-Doubt, Self-Expression, Self-Forgiveness, Self-Harming, Self-Image, Self-Improvement, Self-Inflicted Wound, Self-Interest, Self-Loathing, Self-Made, Self-Pity, Self-Preservation, Self-Reproach, Self-Respect, Self-Righteousness, Self-Sacrifice, Self-Serving Deception, Selfishness, Semantics, Sense, Sense of Loss, Sensible Person, Sensibility, Sensitivity, Share the Load, Shine, Shining Example, Ship, Shouda Woulda Coulda, Shtick, Sickness, Silence, Simple Answer, Simple Pleasure, Simple Question, Simplify, Sitting In the Catbird Seat, Skepticism, Slack, Sleep, Slippery Slope, Slow Play, Small Stuff, Smart Move, Snap Decision, Social Grievance, Soft-Spoken, Solve a Mystery, Sore Wound, Sorrow, Soul, Sound, Sound Purpose, Spark, Speculate, Speechless Real, Spell, Sphere of Influence, Spirited, Spiritual, Spontaneous, Staged Breathing, Staging, Stamina, Stand Down, Stand Up, Star Gaze, Starting Place, Stay, Stay Loose, Stay the Course, Stealth, Steer Away from Pain, Step Up, Stillness, Stimulant, Stingy, Stopping Place, Straight Shooter, Straight-Line Thinker, Strain, Stream of Consciousness, Strength Train, Stress-Coping Mechanisms, Stressor, Strings, Stronger, Struggle, Studied Judgment, Stupid Idea, Stupid Utterance, Stupidity, Subordinate, Substitute, Success, Succinct, Sucker, Sucker Punch, Suffering, Suggestion, Suitable Vice, Superficial Remedy, Superior Course of Action, Superiority Complex, Suppression, Surf, Surprise, Survive, Switch Gears, Sympathy, Synergistic Personality

T
Take a Chance, Take It or Leave It Attitude, Take One's Pleasure, Take the Initiative, Talking Point, Talking To, Test, Tethered,

Thankful, Theist, Thing, Think about the Weight, Think Less, Think More, Thorns in One's Side, Thought, Thrill Seeker, Tide of Events, Tidiness, Tight Place, Time, Timidity, Tipping Point, To-Do List, Token Effort, Tolerate, Tough, Toxic Mix, Toy, Tradition, Traditionalist, Trap, Trash Talk, Travel Light, Trick, Trickster, Trip Wire, Troubles, True Colors, Trust, Truth, Turn Every Which Way but Loose, Tweak, Types of Insults, Types of Motivation

U

Ugliness, Ulterior Motive, Ultimate Question, Unaddressed Problem, Unaffected, Unavoidable Danger, Uncertainty, Under-achiever, Underreact, Understand, Undisciplined, Unenvious, Unfortunate, Unfortunate Jerk, Ungrateful, Unhappiness, Unintended Destination, Uniqueness, Universal Constant, Universe, Unknowable, Unlucky, Unmotivated, Unnecessaries, Unobvious, Unplug, Unreasonable, Unreasonableness, Unstoppable Opponent, Unwelcome Memory, Unworthiness, Upstream Problem, Use Discretion, Utopian

V

Vacation, Vain, Vainglory, Valuable Resource, Verify, Vet, Vexation, Vexed, Vice, Victimize, Victory, Vigorous, Violence, Virtue, Vocabulary

W

Wake Up, Waking, Walk the Talk, Wallow, War, Warning, Wave, Weak Excuse, Weakness, Wealth, Weigh Options, Well-Adjusted, Whole, Why Not Here? Why Not Now?, Wild Hair,

Willfulness, Willingness, Willpower, Wily, Wimpy, Win, Win Goal, Winner's Attitude, Winning Proposition, Wisdom, Wise, Wise Guy, Wise Reserve, Wise Up, Wishful Thinking, Wonder, Word, Work, Working Definition, Worse, Worshiper, Worth of the Stimulation, Wrong, Wrong Action

Y

Yielding

Z

Zero-Sum Effort, Zip It

Descriptions

A

Absolute

A mental finality
A dogmatic conviction of a non-thinker
A standard around which the irrational enthusiastically rally

Absurdity

Ridiculousness
Imparting meaning to the meaningless
Purporting to know the unknowable

Accept

To embrace unconditionally life and what it brings
To calmly wait for the unchangeable to change – *See also Good Fortune*

Accomplishment

The peace of the done

Acknowledgement

The act of recognizing a truth when one stumbles over it – *See also True Colors*

Act One's Age

To moderate one's actions appropriately to compensate for the effects of aging

Action

Life's constant call
The trying that removes the doubt that theory cannot solve

Adapt

To make the best of what each day brings and to gracefully give
up what it has carried away
To change with the changes
To dance to the tune that is played

Addicted to Not Being Addicted

The condition that is a remedy for all compulsions and obsessions
save one

Advantage

A favorable condition that is always accompanied by an unfavorable condition – *See also Disadvantage*

Affected

With pretensions emanating from a perceived superiority to or a
separateness from the universe – *See also Pretension*

Affections

Caring sentiments
The ties that bind

Aftertaste

The taste that reliably tells the tales of good and ill effects

Afterthought

A thought one should have had, but didn't

Age

Times around the sun
Inconclusive evidence of wisdom

Agenda

A plan of action that is aboveboard or devious, obvious or hidden
  – *See also Game Player*

Aggravate an Injury

To make an injury worse by reacting to it rashly – *See also Measured Response*

Aggressively Patient

One who makes a concerted effort to remain calm and capable by suppressing restlessness or annoyance

Agitation

A state of uncomfortable excitement best remedied paradoxically by calm and purposeful endeavors – *See also Grace*

Agnostic

One who professes blissful ignorance of the origin and nature of the universe

Ambiguity

That aspect of reality that negates certainty and dogma, and that
gives rise to doubt, confusion and enlightenment

Ambition

A state of mind devoted to making pipe dreams come true
A ladder against the sky

Amusement

An agreeable occupation that relaxes or entertains
An escape from the harshness and boredom of one's existence –
See also Escapism

Anger

A strong feeling of hostile displeasure that is aroused by a wrong
A feeling state that bites the hand that feeds it – *See also Rash Action*
A feeling state that when well-measured, sharpens the wits, strength-
ens the spirit and excites the body to effective animation

Animosity

Animated ill will

Annoyance

An irritating thing or condition that will not go away on its own
A wearing circumstance

Answer

A pacifying explanation

A pronouncement of fact intended to forestall further inquiry –
See also Fact

A pathway to a more profound question

Anticipate

To make an educated guess about the future – *See also Speculate*

Anxiety

A state of mind that embraces fearful possibilities

Appearance

The superficial aspects of one's person maintained to influence others

Reality's public face – *See also Gullible*

Appeaser

One who yields too easily – *See also Yielding*

Appreciating One's Mortality

Understanding that one may die sooner rather than later

Appropriate Request

Asking for that which is possible for another person to give

Arrogance

A haughty state of mind that underestimates the dangers in happenstance

Arrogant

One imbued with arrogance

One who is reckless and prone to the disasters personally considered unthinkable

One who believes in the illusion of control - See *also Illusion of Control*

One who mistakes power for mastery

Ask for Help

To inform willing rescuers of one's predicament – *See also Share the Load*

Asleep

Residing in the realm of gossamer wings and fairy tales

Asleep at the Wheel

Inappropriately unaware warranting a self-administered swift kick in the posterior

One who knows, but knows not that he knows

Aspire to be Supernatural

To strive to outdo oneself

Atheist

One who does not believe that the universe had a creator

One who does not believe that the universe now has a governing body (an authority figure or figures)

Attend

To create and direct a flow of energy

To listen carefully to what other people say and to observe closely what they do

Attitude

A personal perspective on the condition that one's condition is in

Attractiveness

The quality of being pleasing to others by engendering happiness in them

Authority Figure

A subject matter expert

One with a sheep dog (herder of sheep) mentality

One who holds an intimidating sway over the thoughts and actions of others

Aware

Paying attention – *See also Eyes Wide Open*

Awe

An emotion that is a mix of respect, fear and admiration that is aroused by something that is perceived as extraordinary – *See also Spiritual*

B

Baby Steps
The bite-size pieces of a plan that one can execute easily

Back Off
To retreat, but not give up – *See also Courage*

Bad Action
An action that one undertakes for the hell of it literally
A personally preferred way of making oneself miserable

Bad Attitude
A personal perspective that focuses only on the disadvantageous
  aspects of one's condition

Bad Bargain
A little piece of heaven for a big piece of hell – *See also Good
  Bargain*

Bad Habit
Any habit taken too seriously
A pattern of behavior that one should be well rid of

Bad Memory
A memory that weakens and discourages
A worm hole in space and time to an unreconciled (unsettled) past
A long-suffered remembrance

Bad Request

Asking for the help of one who wishes you ill

Badness

Harming

Baggage

One's useless mental and physical possessions – *See also Travel Light*

Balance

A fluctuating state of physical and mental equilibrium that must compensate for the instabilities of reality by constantly acquiring new centers of gravity – *See also Center of Gravity*

Banish the Thought

To send a thought back to the nothingness from which it came

To classify a thought as irrelevant and therefor unimportant, before it has the opportunity to become rooted in one's stream of consciousness – *See also Classification*

Be Different

To be oneself with daring and do when pressured to be like everyone else – *See also Uniqueness*

Beauty

An inspiring configuration of reality in the eyes of the beholder

A quality of proportion not to be mistaken for truth or profundity or moral goodness

Whatever makes an impression on the heart
seems lovely to the eye.
Sa'di

Behave

To act in reasonable ways when it is self-serving to do so – *See also Misbehave*

Behavior

One's overt reactions to the obvious, the unobvious and the unknowable

Being Easy On Oneself

Harshly and exclusively blaming circumstances or others when one should rightly share in the blame

Being Fair with Oneself

Understanding that one should not and cannot take sole responsibility for anything (good or bad) that happens, and that circumstances (of which one is only an ingredient in the mix) are always the sole determiners of everything that happens.

Being Hard On Oneself

Harshly and exclusively blaming oneself when circumstances or others should rightly share in the blame

Being Human

Personally accepting that one is mortal, vulnerable and imperfect

Belief

A personal supposition, good or bad, about an aspect of one's
existence

Belief System

A nexus (an interconnected and interdependent array) of beliefs
Bottled moonshine
A house of cards

Bend

To adaptively flex – *See also Sag*
To use gentleness and time to grapple with difficulties

Best Apology

A corrective measure

Best Solution

The solution that one routinely finds in the tense space between
opposing ideas
An intelligent choice

Best Trick

The trick that serves its purpose well – *See also Trick*

Better

Exhibiting a comparative advantage in the eye of the beholder
that may actually be a comparative disadvantage if better is on
the way to worse – *See also Worse*

Big Stuff

Aggregated small stuff

Birth

The emergence of a viable (life-sustaining) complexity

Bitched

Adversely affected by the absurdity of the universe without knowingly contributing to the absurdity – *See also Suffering*

A downside to being a hero – *See also Hero*

Bitterness

A strong feeling of resentment that is particularly resistant to the
ameliorative effects of time

A disagreeable feeling state that effectively stimulates one to undertake a vengeful action

Deep-seated (ingrained) anger

Blame Game

The practice of singling out an individual for criticism
and censure for a failure that the many had their hands in

Bleeding Heart

One who unwisely attempts to sympathize with any unhappy occur-
rence however distant and irrelevant – *See also Maudlin Mind*

Bliss

A state of euphoria that is often indicative of naiveté – *See also
Petted and Pampered*

Bluff

To act strong when one is weak – *See also Slow Play*

Bogged Down

Mired in miserable circumstances that are perceived as unchanging and unchangeable – *See also Hell on Earth*

Boldness

The display of an impossible-to-fail attitude, so that failure becomes a less likely outcome

Bond

A dependency personally maintained for the sake of one's happiness – *See also Sense of Loss*

Bored

Paralyzed by the tediousness of one's circumstances – *See also Motion*

Born

To begin to die

Bottom Line

An undeniable truth

Bravery

A demonstration of courage – *See also Courageous*

Breadcrumb

A prompting

A clue – *See also Clueless*

Break

A failed attempt to bend

Break a Bad Habit

To abandon a bad habit by indulging in a less damaging one

To persistently decrease the frequency, duration or intensity of one's indulgences in a bad habit until it dissipates of its own accord

Break a Spell

To heed a wakeup call

Breakdown

A state of incapacity that results from a gross disregard for one's physical and mental limits

Breakthrough

The insight or action that allows one to overcome a barrier, imagined or real

A eureka moment

Breathe

To inhale and exhale freely and easily to improve one's disposition

To inhale deeply and exhale slowly to steady one's aim and strengthen one's resolve

Buy Time
To manipulate the demands of the present for the sake of gaining time to strengthen one's position

C

Call a Spade a Spade

To be honest with oneself
To be honest with others
To speak the truth as one perceives it

Call a Timeout

To step back and make a more studied judgment

Call Out

To challenge oneself or another – *See also Why Not Here? Why Not Now?*

Calm Down

To disown one's emotive state – *See also Detach*

Calmness

A placid demeanor

Captivity

The steady state of life

Care for Oneself

To like oneself enough to live well and be well

Care Less

To disengage from an offending person or situation – *See also Disengage*

Caterwaul

To utter irritating whines and pleas

Caution

Working with a net

Cautious

Stopping, looking and listening

> In your haste, go slowly.
> With reluctance, go boldly.

Cease and Desist

To immediately stop doing what one is doing, or saying what one
is saying or believing what one is believing

Center of Gravity

That which serves one as a source of support and stability
That which provides one with moral or physical strength, free-
dom of action or the will to act
A core belief

Center Stage

A focal point for praise and criticism
Dissipation

Certain Truth

An oxymoron

Certainty

A state of mind that is unable or unwilling to entertain doubt

One's wholesale discounting of one's doubt, so that one can act decisively

Chain of Events

The intrinsic mandate of the universe that one thing leads to another (always)

Challenge

A difficulty that provides one with the opportunity to prevail marvelously – *See also Shine*

A mountain is always there
For those who need a test.
Steep and silent and with rarefied air,
It winnows out the best.

Change

Fluctuations

Ceaseless motion

Transformations – *See also Universal Constant*

Chaos

The randomness that occurs in the midst of order

Character

One's nature

One's persistent and last good refuge from the hypocritical and high-minded ideals of self-professed saints, and the devious and low-minded expediencies of skulking scoundrels

Charity

The gift given unsolicited when one sees the need – *See also Generous*

Cheap Vice

A behavior with underestimated undesirable consequences

Cheese

The bait that traps one – *See also Tethered*

An invite to a snare

Childish

Fighting maturity in ill-conceived ways

Taking one's successes and failures too seriously

Chinks in the Armor

The vulnerabilities of anything that one considers invincible – *See also Invincible*

Circumstances

Those aspects of reality that rule one's existence

Clarify

To attempt to see one's way clear – *See also One's Path*

Classification

The process that one uses to convert one's experiences into words and numbers

Clean House

To create personal space by getting rid of one's baggage

Cleaning

Moving a disagreeableness from one place to another

Clear Mind

A state of mind that is not affected by exaggerated feelings or misunderstood significances

A mind not cluttered with the memories of one's lesser selves

A state of mind that is capable of seeing one's delusions as the illusions that they are – *See also Delusion*

Cleverness

The ability to advantageously conceal one's intentions while contending with others – *See also Wily*

Closed Book

A life-event that is not open to examination and rumination

Closed-Mindedness

The ability to understand less by refusing to understand more

The disposition to understand everything too soon

A mind closed by belief

Clueless

Displaying an abundance of stupidity
Unable to take promptings from reality
A level of ignorance that is not conducive to a valid opinion

Coast

To advantageously use the favorable momentum generated by one's effort

Coast to the Line

To finish in one's own good time – *See also Free Spirit*

When the race is won,
always another race to run,
coast to the line in your own good time.
And when the race is lost,
at whatever the cost,
coast to the line in your own good time.

Code of Conduct

Rules worth following that one chooses to follow

Cognitive Dissonance

The mental anguish experienced by an individual who holds two or more contradictory beliefs, ideas, or values at the same time, performs an action that is contradictory to one or more beliefs, ideas, or values, or is confronted by new information that conflicts with existing beliefs, ideas, or values

The mental discomfort that motivates one to attempt to resolve the contradictions, conflicts, inconsistencies and vagaries of everyday life

Coherent

Demonstrating the ability to accurately comprehend, to the degree possible, one's circumstances

One who is able to marshal one's mental faculties to the task of understanding

Cold War

A state of hostile coexistence between those with irreconcilable differences

Covert warfare

Colloquialist

One who possesses and uses an informal vocabulary that is composed of words and phrases that are characteristically metaphorical, playful, elliptical, vivid, whimsical and ephemeral

A slang master

Collywobbles

The nervousness occasioned by the occasion – *See also Anxiety*

A case of the jitters

Comeback

The act of regaining one's former stature through hard work and good fortune – *See also Knockdown*

To get up after being knocked down

Comeuppance

Negative consequences that one incurs as rightful retribution for a past action – *See also Karmic Justice*

Sitting down to a course of consequences

Just desserts

Compartmentalization

Refusing to consciously consider one's conflicting ideas, values or beliefs, because to do so would damage one's sense of personal wholeness and sincerity (i.e. to bring into question one's integrity) – *See also Cognitive Dissonance*

Avoiding cognitive dissonance at all cost

Compassionate

Willing to help others, because they need the help

Competition

A struggle between determined opponents for the sake of a rewarding experience

Competitor

One who plays a game to win

Complacency

A state of contentment and self-satisfaction that no station in life supports – *See also Safety*

Complain

To express dissatisfaction with the condition that one's condition
    is in

To protest one's circumstances without duly noting that they
    could be worse

> I was complaining that I had no shoes
> till I met a man who had no feet.
> *Confucius*

Complexity

Any complex thing or system having properties and functions
    determined not only by the properties and relations of its in-
    dividual parts, but by the character of the whole that they
    compose and by the relations of the parts to the whole

A whole that is greater than the sum of its parts – *See also Whole*

Composure

Grace under fire

Comprehend

To grasp the nature, significance or meaning of an event

To personally own an idea

Compulsion

An irresistible urge

Con

A lie
Spin
A slant

> You can fool all of the people some of the time,
> and some of the people all of the time,
> but you cannot fool all of the people all of the time.
> *Abraham Lincoln*

Con (2)

To put forth a seemingly believable but fraudulent scheme with
the intent to swindle the gullible

To put forth a scheme that traffics in fanciful future rewards while
adversely affecting present realities

Concentrate

To make the field of thought so small that there is no room for
fear, pain or any thought other than the accomplishment of
a narrow purpose

Concern

The anxious feeling that arises from a perceived threat to a valued
bond

Conformist

A team player

One who embraces groupthink (the uncritical acceptance of the
ideas, values or beliefs of a group)

One who is prone to fawning, flattering and pandering

A known quantity

Confusion

A state of mental disorganization that is frequently more valuable than a state of mental organization – *See also Conviction*

Congregation

A group of people who share the same belief system – *See also Belief System*

A flock

A tribe

A support group

Consequences

The obvious effects of a thought or action, projected or realized, that one uses to make a logical assumption about the thought or action – *See also Logic*

The results of a thought or action that are essential for determining meaning, truth and value

Conservative

One who will not embrace or promote change

A champion of the status quo

A traditionalist

An unwilling adopter of new ideas

Consider

To carefully think again before one acts

Construct

To bring elements or parts together by arrangement or combination

Contempt

A disrespectful and disdainful attitude that is particularly useful when dealing with the despicable

Contentment

A temporary state of calm that abides at one's center

Contradictions

Inconsistencies that are invariably present

Contrarian

One who enjoys quarreling

Conviction

An unshakeable belief that is prone to all of the shortcomings of certainty and closed-mindedness
A strongly held belief that can be a dangerous enemy of truth

Convinced

An in-the-know state of mind

Cooler

A harmful event that is unavoidable
A damaging blow to one's enthusiasm

Cooperate

To work together to achieve a common benefit

To make life less difficult for each other

Core Belief

A strongly held belief around which one's actions and thoughts happily or unhappily congregate

Core Beliefs

Nothing in the universe is worthy of worship (even the universe itself is not worthy of flattering, fawning and pandering) – *See also Universe*

There are aspects of reality that will be forever excluded from one's perceptions of reality – *See also Unknowable*

There is no thing in the universe that is whole and of one piece – *See also God Particle*

Courage

The ability to judge that something else is more important than fear

The ability to face intimidating facts without flinching

The ability to run away when the day is lost

Courageous

Displaying a willingness to confront, to overcome and to use to one's advantage one's fear

Getting out by going through

Coward

One who is excessively fearful of one's circumstances

Cowardice

A state of mind that is unable or unwilling to react constructively to life's difficulties

Creation

The unknowable process that makes something out of nothing

Creativity

Constructively or deconstructively playing with circumstances
Daydreaming (dreaming while awake)

Criteria for Belief or Disbelief

Some credible evidence
A preponderance of circumstantial (seemingly relevant) evidence
Specific (highly relevant and detailed) evidence

Criticism

Justified unkindness

Crook

One who traffics in ulterior motives – *See also Deceiver*

Crutch

That which helps make bearable the unbearable

Cunning

Skilled at deception – *See also Trickster*
One who is adept at setting traps – *See also Trap*

Curiosity

A strong desire to learn or know something
Nosiness

Cynic

One who ascribes his own mean motives to others
One who traffics in dark truths – *See also Dark Truth*

D

Dangerous Living

A stimulating lifestyle
A daring adventure

Dangerous Rhetoric

Empty talk that incites

Dangling

A state of perilous suspension that to remedy requires a helping hand up or the personal initiative to get down on one's own

Daring

A reckless disregard for danger — *See also Unavoidable Danger*

Dark Truth

A disagreeable reality that utopians strive to obscure so that their dogmatic beliefs can continue to flourish unabated

Darkly Recalcitrant

Preferring ideas and actions that fly in the face of one's duty to reason — *See also Unreasonableness*

Dead and Buried

That which has been committed to the irrefutable past

Jim Boyd

The Moving Finger writes; and, having writ,
Moves on: nor all thy Piety nor Wit
Shall lure it back to cancel half a Line,
Nor all thy Tears wash out a Word of it.
Omar Khayyám

Dead-End

A blind alley
An activity that has no redeeming qualities
Pain without gain

Deadhead

One who wholeheartedly pursues a dead-end

Death

Game over
The absence of life's constraints – *See also Captivity*
That which exists between the end of one life and the beginning
of another

Death rearranges the world
For the living and the dead.
And one always wonders
Why the other went ahead.

Debacle

A ludicrous failure of intelligence that defies description – *See also
Disgusting*

Deceiver

One who encourages ill-founded beliefs
One who regards deception as a necessary evil
A shyster — *See also Crook*

Deception

A cleverly rendered lie
A dishonest action that is tiresome and worrisome for the one
engaging in it

Decide

To become conscious of a conclusion that one has reached unconsciously
To reach a conclusion because one is tired of thinking about the
alternatives

Decide Not to Decide

To make a decision not to make a decision, because it is advantageous to do so

Deconstruct

To take apart something (a thing, an idea, an event, a doctrine, etc.) in order to examine and think about its parts
(elements)

Defeat

A temporary victory for the opposition and not the final word on
anything — *See also Knockdown*

Deference

A submissive attitude – *See also Obedience*

Defiant

Standing one's ground

> Now I know the things I know,
> And do the things I do;
> And if you do not like me so,
> To hell my love with you.
> *Dorothy Parker*

Delayed Reactions

One's perceptions of reality

Delightful Occupations

Playful activities that are pointedly disrespectful of the sham seriousness of life – *See also Play for Fun*

> Taking fun
> as only fun
> and earnestness
> in earnest
> shows how thoroughly
> thou none
> of the two
> discernest.
> *Piet Hein*

Delusion

An illusion that one takes seriously

Demagogue

One who manipulates others by appealing to their irrational fears and prejudices
One who gives a voice and a helping hand to the worst in others
A rabble-rouser

Demands of the Day

One's priorities for the day that appropriately discount the priorities of others — *See also Discipline*

Demerit

A milestone in a self-debilitating process
A disadvantage added to one's sum total of disadvantages
A victory for a lesser self

Demon

A vexed self — *See also Vexation*

Dent

To weaken an obstacle
Meaningful, but precarious progress — *See also Progress*

Dependencies

Persistent connections

Dependency

One's reliance upon a crutch – *See also Crutch*

Dependent

Exhibiting the inability to stand on one's own two feet defiantly when frightened and alone

Derelict

One who is adrift and powerless – *See also Ineffectualness*

Desire

A strong feeling that impels one to attain or possess something

A reason to be (raison d'etre)

A locomotive – *See also Driven*

Despair

A state of hopelessness that can make one a trembling fool with its dark exaggerations

Detach

To disengage from one's feeling or emotion when one's feeling or emotion serves no good purpose – *See also Calm Down*

Deterioration

A measurable change for the worse

A gradual decline into chaos

Die

To begin to be born

Differences of Opinion

Conflicting opinions with varying degrees of separation from the truth that are instigators of competitions and conflicts

Difficulty

The adversity that one must stand up to, so that it may stand down

Diminishment

The demise of one's friend or one's enemy

Have you learned lessons only of those
who admired you, and were tender with you,
and stood aside for you?
Have you not learned the great lessons
of those who rejected you
and braced themselves against you?
or who treated you with contempt,
or disputed the passage with you?
Walt Whitman

Dimwit

One who continues to believe that he (she) is right despite compelling evidence to the contrary — *See also Hard Head*

Direct Question

A question that one asks with open disdain for the unwelcome answer that it will elicit

A question that deserves a straight answer

Dirt

A disagreeableness that one moves from one place to another
That which immediately begins to accumulate when one stops cleaning

Disadvantage

An unfavorable condition that is always accompanied by a favorable condition – *See also Advantage*

Disambiguation

Removing, to the extent possible, the ambiguity (vagueness) of a situation by focusing one's thoughts and actions upon verifying its unambiguous (obvious) aspects
To take a person, a thing, an idea, a doctrine or a situation at face value

Disappointment

A feeling of dissatisfaction that results from an unrealized expectation

Disbelief

An initial state of healthy skepticism, when one is confronted by new information that conflicts with one's existing beliefs, ideas, or values
An unhealthy state of persistent skepticism that prevents one from accepting a truth, good or bad, about an aspect of one's existence

Discipline

Behavior that is in accord with a goal-driven commitment
Doing one's first things first

Discourage

To dampen one's enthusiasm or the enthusiasm of another with pessimism – *See also Pessimism*

Disengage

To free oneself from a commitment

To stop caring

Disgusting

Repulsive to one's intellect and sensibilities

Dishonor

A weak commitment to right belief and action

Disinterestedness

Stillness in response to motives

Dismiss a Thought

To allow a thought to dissipate by not embellishing it

Disown

To sever intellectual, emotional or physical ties

To refuse to continue to be associated with a person, an action, a thought, a value or a belief

Displaced Aggression

Focusing one's anger and hostility on a soft target (a person or thing that cannot retaliate effectively) instead of the intimidating hard target that is the true object of one's anger and hostility

Distillate

The impure product of a reductionist process that is sold to the unwary as pure – *See also Essence*

Distracted

Not engaged with the present moment

Do Less

To think more

Do More

To think less

Do the Deed

To transform an intention into an action

Do the Math

To use numbers to better understand one's circumstances

Dogma

An illogical assertion of certainty about that which is fundamentally uncertain

A conviction without tolerance

A belief system that is not evidence-based

Done Deal

An understanding that emerges into one's consciousness as definitive and conclusive

Don't Know. Don't Care.

A proper send-off for niggling curiosity

Doubt

A judicious sense of what not to believe

To show proper respect for that which one does not know

To react to inconsistencies that one senses, but does not necessarily comprehend

To show proper disrespect for that which one knows

Doubter

One worthy of doubting

Drama

All of life's sound and fury that has no lasting significance

A tempest in a teapot

Draw a Line in the Sand

To create an arbitrary boundary between the acceptable and the unacceptable

Dream

A fantasy played to an audience of one

Dreamer

One who entertains fanciful notions

A wellspring of new ideas

An agent of progress

Driven

Motivated to do one's own bidding

Dust

The particulars associated with an event that eventually lump together and settle – *See also Event*

Fallout

Duty

A rationalization for doing someone else's bidding – *See also Demands of the Day*

Dysfunctional Thought

A thought that works against one's best interest – *See also Stupid Idea*

E

Easy Answer

The answer that is reliably neat, plausible and wrong
An explanation that provides a non-thinker with blissful refuge
from reasonable doubt

Easy Rider

One who sits light in the saddle with slack in the reins

Easy Street

A temporarily abundant state of being that one should enjoy
while it lasts – *See also Sitting in the Catbird Seat*
Easy come. Easy go.
Gain without pain

Easy Way

The course of action taken when there is no obvious advantage in
doing something a harder way
The path of least resistance

Edges of a Problem

Those aspects of a problem that one addresses until one can get to
the heart of it – *See also Heart of the Problem*

Educate Oneself

To contend with one's ignorance by daring to learn – *See also
Follow*

Effective

Well-equipped with and proficient in using one's own devices

Efficient

Making the least amount of effort go the longest way

Effort

The exertion needed to get something done – *See also Life Cycle of an Effort*

Elephant in the Room

An aspect of reality that one has great difficulty acknowledging
The unknowable

Elevate One's Game

To improve one's circumstances and collaterally oneself
To improve oneself and collaterally one's circumstances

Emotional Intelligence

To pay attention to how one feels, so that one's feelings can be knowingly incorporated into one's thoughts and actions
To assess how others feel, so that these assessments can duly affect one's behavior

Emotional Sobriety

A state of mind that gives one's feelings and emotions, and the feelings and emotions of others the respect that they deserve

A state of mind that sees one's feelings and emotions for what they are (motivators of the first order, and powerful usurpers of reasoned behavior and rational argument)

Emotive State
A mental state in which one's emotions usurp one's volitional and cognitive functions

Empathy
The ability to put oneself in the frame of reference of another living thing

Imaginatively putting oneself in another person's shoes to better understand his or her situation

To imaginatively feel what another living thing feels

A prerequisite for a sympathetic reaction

Empower Oneself
To act on what one believes to be right and in doing so to disdain what one considers to be trick and duplicity – *See also Hero*

To call upon one's resources to rid oneself of a vexation – *See also Exorcise*

Emptiness
The antagonist that inspires all effort

An opportunity to pursue fulfillment

Encourage
To bolster one's enthusiasm or the enthusiasm of another with optimism – *See also Optimism*

End of Day
The trough of the day that is the precursor to a new day
The time of the day when one should not undertake important matters

Endeavor
An activity that one engages in willingly or unwillingly

Enduring Sentiment
Lasting sweetness or bitterness – *See also Nostalgia*

Enemy
One who wishes you ill
Anyone or anything that has harmed you or intends to harm you
One who has chosen to oppose you in all matters
Food for thought – *See also Diminishment*

Engage Life
To purposefully and actively live
To take the bull by the horns

Enjoy Life
To enjoy the struggle and the rewards that come from one's struggling

Enjoy the Scenery
To enjoy the setting of one's life – *See also Simple Pleasure*
To enjoy the place where one stands

Enlightenment

Understanding that one's understandings are always
suspect (worthy of doubt)

Knowing that one cannot know anything entire (with no elements or parts left out)

Enough Is Enough

The judgment that continuing to do what one is doing makes no
sense – *See also Futility*

Entertainment

An activity that one takes part in as an observer or a participant
that grabs one's attention and holds one interest

An activity that promotes the acknowledgement and the free expression of one's feelings and emotions

A captivating experience

Enthusiasm

The exalted feeling that results from seeing one's favored purpose
as possible

Happily squandering oneself for a purpose

Envious

One who is unable to say the words, "I'd rather be me.", and mean
them

Escapism

The practice of freeing oneself from the routines and rigors of
one's life through amusements

Essence
The irreducible nature of a thing – *See also Purity*

Etching
An event that one remembers well
An indelible memory

Event
A phenomenon appearing to be located at a single point in space
and time that only a fool believes has fixed boundaries that
are clearly understandable and controllable

Ever-Growing Calm
The pleasing effect that comes from abandoning, once and for all,
a futile hope – *See also Give Up*

Evidence
Grounds for believing or not believing a hypothesis
Grounds for partially believing and partially not believing a
hypothesis

Evil
A harmful intention or action that escalates insipidly unless con-
tended with
Not playing nice
One who derives pleasure from willfully hurting others

Evolution
Replication, variation, competition, selection

An Uncommon Vocabulary (4th Edition Revised)

Exaggerate

To make what is easy seem difficult

To make the trivial seem important – *See also Hype*

Excitement

A state of heartfelt invigoration

Excuse

A rationale (often contrived) for one's behavior

Exercise in Futility

An activity that results in short-term happiness, but delivers longer-term unhappiness

Adorning an ignoble person with noble sentiments – *See also Noble Pretensions of Ignoble Persons*

Seeking sufficiency in an insufficient universe

Exhaustion

A state of severely depleted physical and mental resources

Exist

To travel the road between nowhere and everywhere – *See also One's Path*

> With them the seed of wisdom did I sow
> And with my own hand labored it to grow
> And this was all the harvest that I reaped
> I came like water, and like wind I go.
> *Omar Khayyám*

Exonerate
To relieve oneself of guilt through good actions remembered or undertaken

Exorcise
To rid oneself of a vexation

Experience
A bank account of useful memories
Lessons learned

Experiment
A process for verifying the justifying premises of one's hypothetical conclusion – *See also Test*

Explicit Thought
A state of mind that focuses upon those aspects of reality that are open to conceptualization and quantification, and that exist independently of the observer – *See also Holistic Thought*

Explicit You
The comprehensible you
One's aspects that can be conceptualized or quantified

Explore
To make known the unknown
To go from the known to the unknown with one's eyes open

Externally Validate

To give form and substance to one's idea to see if it can stand on
its own two feet in the world of things

To try one's ideas on others to see if they create good effects

To expose one's ideas to the whims and vagaries of other human
beings

Extremism

Intolerant idealism – *See also Idealism*

Eyes Wide Open

A state of mental alertness that allows one to see circumstances
change, as they are wont to do – *See also Sense*

F

Facilitate

To do something in such a way as to make the doing of another thing easier

To grease the skids

Fact

A simplified explanation of complex phenomena that a simple mind can take comfort in – *See also Easy Answer*

A component of a truth

Fail Forward

To pursue success by using lessons learned the hard way

Failed Experiment

Results that negate the validity of an idea

Failure

A design unsuccessfully realized in the eyes of the beholder

An unfavorable result that can create feelings of guilt and remorse

A failing that is open to question and not exclusively a logical outcome

The agony of defeat – *See also Defeat*

A breeding ground for success (if one learns from one's mistakes)

Fair Price

A favorable outcome for both sides in a negotiation – *See also Lasting Agreement*

Jim Boyd

Faith
A feel-good belief system – *See also Belief System*

Faithful
Those persons who are dogmatic about their dogmas

Fall Off the Wagon
To return to a previously harmful state, practice or belief

False Prophet
One who knows the unknowable, and who is capable of motivating others with this knowledge

Fanciful Notion
A pipe dream that usually benefits one little

> Dreams are the subtle Dower
> That make us rich an Hour –
> Then fling us poor
> Out of the purple door.
> *Emily Dickinson*

Far Side
That which one focuses upon when the near side is too discouraging
The longer view – *See also Near Side*

Faster
Bolder – *See also Hurry*

Fate

Given the confluent (flowing together) nature of circumstances, what happens must happen, and what does not happen cannot happen — *See also Go with the Flow*

Que sera, sera. (What will be, will be.)

Fathom

To plumb the depths of reality in search of certainty

Fatigue

A state of tiredness that compels one to review the worth of the actions that are producing it

Fear

The hysterical messenger that one should dismiss after it has delivered its alarming message

Fear Monger

One who uses fear as a means to an end

A merchant of fear

Fearless Leader

The leader who ignorantly leads others into danger, and whose direction is not worth following

Fed Up

Sick and tired of the way things are

Annoyed to the point of being motivated to change

Fight

A brutal, gut-rending test of wills and courage that requires one to be combative and to give no quarter to one's opponent – *See also Violence*

A pugnacious encounter

Final Answer

The Theory of Everything (TOE)

The realization that there is not a final answer to anything

An impossible-to-attain state of certainty

Find One's Way

To make ongoing and honest assessments of one's abilities, interests and nature, and to find and occupy niches that match these assessments – *See also Niche*

Finish

To reach the end of a charted course – *See also Stopping Place*

To cross the finish line

First Good Step in Addressing the Present

To discount the future

First Good Step in Breaking a Harmful Habit

To draw a line in the sand

First Good Step in Forgetting the Past

To be open to the present

First Good Step in Helping Oneself

To believe in one's worthiness for the help

First Good Step in Making an Adjustment

To believe in one's ability to adjust

First Good Step in Preparing for the Future

To illuminate the past

First Good Step in Pursuing Happiness

To realize that taking one's circumstances seriously is optional

First Principle

A rule derived from a core belief

Flight

An escape strategy that offers no lasting protection against unhappiness

Flinching

Demonstrating weakness or fright – *See also Courage*

Flip Side

The opposing position that is often equivalently advantageous

Fly by the Seat of One's Pants

To learn as one goes

Focus
To bring one's thoughts and actions to bear

Follow
To understand

Follow the Breadcrumbs
To take promptings from reality however irrelevant they may seem

Follower
One who teaches himself the things that other people know
One who is willing to follow (understand)
One who knows not, and knows that he knows not

Fool
One who bases thought and action upon ill-founded beliefs
One who is particularly adept at failing
One who believes that he is wise in all matters
One who knows not and knows not that he knows not

Foolhardy
Exposing oneself unnecessarily to danger or loss
One who squanders his share of luck or merit on foolishness

Foolish Thrift
A commitment to thrift that encourages one to stop living today
for the sake of living well tomorrow

An Uncommon Vocabulary (4th Edition Revised)

Foolishness
An ill-founded belief

Forethought
The act of considering likely consequences and future states

Forget
To acquire new memories to replace the old
To remedy one's sadness and bitterness with unmindfulness

Forget Time
To take no notice of time at all

Forgive
To reach a level of understanding or compassion for an offender
that is sufficient to quell one's desire for revenge

Forgiveness
The appropriate pardoning of another person when that person
has sufficiently suffered
The benevolent sentiment that is useful in ameliorating a futile
desire for revenge
The refusal to further embrace thoughts of revenge, because they
are damaging to oneself

Fortunate
Having the good luck to be in the right place at the right time
with the abilities necessary to benefit from the situation

Reaping benefits from going in the right direction for the wrong reasons

Fortune
The pendulum that swings to and fro from light to dark, and high to low
The wheel that takes one up and down in turn

Frame of Reference
The sum total of the conditions that affect one's perceptions of reality at a given moment in time
A mental construct of how things are

Free
Not constrained by slavish devotions to virtue or vice

Free Spirit
One who spends one's life in one's own way, and as a consequence spends it well – *See also Happiness*
One who lives life at one's own pace and steers by one's own charts – *See also Navigate*

Free Will
The misconception that one's behavior emanates from sources that are knowable in some ultimate and final way, and therefore are consciously controllable in some ultimate and final way – *See also Self-Control*

Friend

One who wishes you well – *See also Bond*
A support group of one

Friendly Game

A competition in which the competitors use kid gloves and rubber swords – *See also Kid Gloves*

Frustration

The annoyance that results from encountering a stubborn obstacle
A crisis in self-esteem

Fulfillment

A temporary state of satisfaction

Fully Engaged

Purposefully emotional

Fun

Doing what one enjoys

Futility

The ineffectiveness that results from pursuing doggedly a design that is not realizable
A state of ineffectualness that requires for its amelioration changing or abandoning an errant design
A fundamentally frustrating property of existence – *See also Exercise in Futility*

Future
Upcoming events that routinely elude seeing, shaping and stopping from happening
Speculation
A carrot on a stick

Fuzziness
Persistent ambiguity
The fundamental vagueness of everything

Fuzzy Rule
A rule with the latitude to take into account recurring measures of relevant circumstances

Fuzzy Thinking
Thinking that embraces ambiguity and uncertainty, and that rejects out of hand absolutes and certitudes

Fuzzy Universe
This incomprehensible universe that superficially presents itself as comprehensible and determinable

G

Gain Insight
To discover what one is running from and to, and why

You and me,
We pursue and flee.
And always we wonder why.
How can that be, asked he?
To be born is to begin to die, said I.
And therein lies the rub.

Gain Traction
To enhance one's ability to affect one's circumstances – *See also Elevate One's Game*

Game
A contest that is aboveboard or devious governed by a set of obvious or unobvious rules

Game Player
One who seduces others into playing his or her game according to his or her rules
One who plays a devious game by unobvious rules

General Order of Things
The state of things that is well equipped with and proficient in using its own devices
The regularities of life

Generalize

To produce an idea that is gross enough to be true

To produce an idea that is gross enough to be false

Generous

Helpful to others at some cost to oneself

Genuineness

Being oneself, and thinking and acting accordingly – *See also Integrity*

That which abides where there is artificiality and masks

Get

To acquire something by giving up something immediately or in the long run

Get a Grip

To reach out for something to hold on to

Tying a knot and hanging on when one gets to the end of one's rope

Get Back in the Saddle

To return to a previously challenging behavior or situation (particularly if the going back requires significant personal fortitude)

Get One's Blood Up

To enter an emotive state – *See also Emotive State*

Get Real

To stop taking fanciful notions seriously – *See also Fanciful Notion*

Gift

An outward expression of one's sincere good will

Give the Benefit of the Doubt

To temper one's negative emotional response by entertaining alternative explanations of offending circumstances

To attribute to stupidity that which one first apprehends as malice

Give Up

To abandon hope and effort as the result of a good measure of sense

To consent to the obstructions of reality

Give-Up in the Get

The price of doing business – *See also Price*

Glutton

One who cannot get enough of a good thing

One who considers greed a virtue

Glutton for Punishment

One who refuses to learn from painful experiences

Glutton's Punishment

Too much of a good thing

Go with the Flow

To swim with the tide
To get with the program

Goal

An attractive possibility
An imaginary future

God Particle

An imaginary oneness
The holy grail of a reductionist

Going the Extra Mile

Exceeding one's expectations or the expectations of others by going beyond what is required

Good Action

An action that results in lasting happiness for oneself that one undertakes for the pleasure of it

Good Attitude

A personal perspective that focuses only on the advantageous aspects of one's condition – *See also Wealth*

Good Bargain

A little piece of hell for a big piece of heaven

Good Communication

A marrying of wit and sense
Free speech worth listening to

Good Decision

A decision based upon the right consideration of pertinent influences – *See also Intelligence*

Good Enough

Sufficient to meet a need without further improvement – *See also Practicality*

Good Fortune

The ability to endure misfortune with grace – *See also Grace*

Good Journey

One with a safe arrival

Good Memory

A memory that strengthens and encourages
A worm hole in space and time to a reconciled (settled) past
A soothing tonic for one's present ailments

Good Request

A reasonable request made of a friend – *See also Friend*

Good Riddance

A fond farewell to a vexation

Goodness

A demonstration of kindness and benevolence that encourages one's friends and confuses one's enemies

Helping

Playing nice

Grace

The ability to remain calm and capable when one encounters difficulty, pain, delay or incongruity

Graceful

Capable of easily navigating life's real and imagined obstacles

Grasping at Straws

To entertain a desperate plan that has little hope of success

Greedy

Given to plundering for the sake of plundering

One who aspires to gluttony

Grief

An overwhelming sense of loss – *See also Sense of Loss*

Grieving Process

The transformation of one's grief into thoughts, words and actions, so that one can leave it behind in a changed state – *See also Stress-Coping Mechanisms*

Grinder

One who willingly embraces significant hardships in the pursuit of a personally difficult goal

One who is willing to do the work (however tedious) that is necessary to be successful

Grounded

Well-versed in one's abilities, interests and nature

Growth Hormone

A leap in the dark

An unpremeditated act

Guilt

Remorse for one's action or inaction

Mental anguish that is well-suited to those of us who believe that they control circumstances

Gullible

Easily deceived by glitter and tarnish – *See also Appearance*

H

Habit
A pattern of behavior that is comfortable and comforting to repeat

Half-Truth
A truth that is less true than a whole truth
A partial truth
A foundation for an effective lie

Hangover
The sum total of the ill effects to oneself that result from indulging in a vice – *See also Pay the Piper*

Happiness
Saying one's say and having one's day, and leaving it at that – *See also Free Spirit*
The feeling state that accompanies a successful experiment
A state of diminished unhappiness
The aftertaste of a good action

Happiness and Unhappiness
Feeling states that are involuntary reactions to one's perceptions of one's circumstances as improving or worsening respectively

Harass
To effectively irritate an adversary lest he be at ease to carry on with his malevolent designs – *See also Off-Balance Opponent*

Hard Head

One who knows only when he has suffered

Hard Rider

One who seeks out hard lessons
One who is aggressively stupid

Hard Way

The course of action taken when there is no easier way – *See also*
    Strength Train
A rocky road

Harm

The hurt that undeceives

> I have no fund of tears to weep
> for the happenings that undeceive.
> *Paul Laurence Dunbar*

Harmony

A persistent alignment and sympathy between one's thoughts,
    words and actions – *See also Integrity*
A lasting agreement between the man and the life that he leads
At peace with oneself

Harshness

An appropriately severe reaction to obvious disrespect or blatant
    stupidity

Hate

To intensely dislike something

Hateful

One who deserves to be intensely disliked

Having One's Day

To do the things that need doing
To explore, engage and enjoy life

Heal from the Inside Out

To keep a sore wound open and sore, and to treat it daily with
generous doses of gentle, disinfecting reality until it heals
from the inside out

Health

A goodly state of mind and body that one pursues when one tires
of being ill and malcontent

Heart of Hearts

Where one's feelings come together and get sorted out
The final authority on the rightness or wrongness of one's action
and thought

Heart of the Problem

Those aspects of a problem that one needs to address to solve the
problem
The root causes

Heart of Things

A field of infinite potential
The nothingness that conjures up reality

At the heart of things,
You will find nothing hiding there.
Care and in caring
Loose the healing fountain flow
To green the desert of your despair.

Heaven on Earth

The thrill of victory
The excitement and delight that accompanies a eureka moment –
    See also Breakthrough
An experience to die for (figuratively speaking)

Men talk of heaven, - there is no heaven but here;
Men talk of hell, - there is no hell but here;
Men of hereafters talk and future lives,
O love, there is no other life - but here.
Omar Khayyám

Hell on Earth

The agony of defeat
The sum total of the barriers, real and imagined, that curtail one's
    abilities to explore, engage and enjoy life – *See also Bogged Down*
An experience to live through – *See also Courageous*

Here and Now

Not there and then (ever again)

Hero

An empowered self – *See also Empower Oneself*

Hero Worship

To value a hero too highly

Hide and Seek

The game that insidious chaos always wins – *See also Deterioration*

High-Yield Investment

Kindness

Higher Self

A more principled self – *See also Principled*
A self that demonstrates a strong commitment to right belief and
action – *See also Honor*

Hindsight

The ability to look at the past and claim the illusionary benefit of
20/20 vision

History

Imperfect recollections that are always a mix of the old with the
new

Holistic Thought

A state of mind that perceives reality as a continuum, a whole, a process that eludes conceptualization and quantification, and that subsumes the observer – *See also Unaffected*

Honesty

The ability to stretch out lies over time, distance and circumstance, until they dissipate of their own accord

Making the smallest amount of lying go the longest way

Honor

A strong commitment to right belief and action

Hope

To feel that something wished for will happen

Hot Head

One who is particularly susceptible to emotive states

One who is unable to remain calm and capable when faced with difficulty, pain, delay or incongruity

Human Being

A creature that is an accumulation of animated stardust with an attitude

A creature that is an ordering of matter that supports self-consciousness

An organism among countless organisms – *See also Organism*

Humanist

One who believes that human needs and interests are more important than philosophical, theological or ideological ideals

Humanity

An insignificant experiment involving the capacities to feel and to reason that is taking place in a vast universe that overwhelmingly thinks not and cares not

Humility

The capacity to remember how far one has come with so little and how quickly one can return to where one has come from

The honest assessment of one's personal significance – *See also Humanity*

Humor

Wit that amuses

Hunger

A compelling desire

Hunker Down

To get out of harm's way

Hurry

To hasten too quickly

Hype

A self-serving exaggeration
An extravagant claim of worth or worthlessness
Using big words for small matters

Hypocrite

One who speaks well, but acts poorly
One who feigns goodness – *See also Noble Pretensions of Ignoble Persons*

Hypothesis

An idea for testing – *See also Test*

I

Idea

A physiological, psychological and sociological artifact that is infinitely mutable

A peg to hang an action on

Ideal

The imperfect conception of something in its absolute perfection

A fairy tale

A myth

Idealism

A doctrine that elevates blindly the pursuit of an ideal, and that grossly ignores those aspects of reality that refuse to be subsumed within the doctrine

A doctrine that can be a motivator for, and a justifier of human malice and stupidity – *See also Extremism*

Idealist

One who wholeheartedly pursues an ideal

Ideals

The stuff that aspirations are made of

Idiocy

Extreme stupidity – *See also Debacle*

Idiot

One who is extremely stupid

Ignorance

An uninformed state of mind

Illegitimate Suffering

To suffer without attempting to remedy one's suffering

Illusion

A false perception, idea or belief

Illusion of Control

The delusion that one can attain success by controlling in some definite and final way the contributions of favorable circumstances

The delusion that one can avoid failure by controlling in some definite and final way the interventions of unfavorable circumstances

Imagine

To create a reality with one's thoughts

Impactful

Able to make a significant dent – *See also Progress*

Imperfection

A persistent flaw in this otherwise perfect universe

That which immediately begins to manifest itself when one stops pursuing perfection

Impetus Behind Evolution

The innate capacity of the universe to exponentially grow populations of replicators (self-replicating molecules, cells and multi-cellular entities) — *See also Evolution*

Implicit Thought

A state of mind that focuses upon the theoretical (hypothetical) rather than the demonstrable

Postulating

Inferential thinking

Implicit You

The incomprehensible you

One's aspects that can be speculated about (inferred), but not ascertained

Impossible

Not able to be done even when appearing doable — *See also Possible*

Improve Oneself

To give up vices — *See also Vice*

To accrue virtues — *See also Virtue*

To indulge one's vices less and one's virtues more

Indecision

A condition of agitated incapacity that when present ensures that a worthy endeavor will fail

Independent

The ability to stand on one's own two feet defiantly when frightened and alone

Having the courage of one's convictions

Indiscretion

A necessary indulgence in excessive risk-taking to ameliorate the effects of boredom

Individualized Accomplishment

An over-simplified assessment of a successful endeavor that does not justly acknowledge the contributions of others – *See also Self-Made*

Individualized Guilt

An over-simplified assessment of a failed or hurtful endeavor that one uses to justify punishing oneself or others – *See also Blame Game*

Indulge

To take advantage of an affordable or unaffordable opportunity to pursue one's happiness – *See also Take One's Pleasure*

Ineffectualness

A personal commitment to weakness and inconsistency – *See also Wimpy*

Embraced helplessness

Inertia

The tendency to maintain one's current course even when a change of course is called for

Inferior Opponent

An opponent who is vulnerable to simple traps
An opponent in the midst of making a mistake

Inferiority Complex

A personal appraisal that undervalues one's strengths and talents

Influence

Overt or covert manipulation

A wink
And a clink
Will get you more
Than you think.

Information

The fabric of reality
The tail that wags the dog

Innovate

To find new ways to arrange or combine old things

Insanity

The inability to behave normally
Minimized normality – *See also Sanity*

Inspiration

A motivating idea that puts a bounce in one's step and a sparkle in one's eye

A state of mind that embraces a promising possibility

Instinct

One's innate ability to cope with one's circumstances

One's first and best line of defense

Insubordination

Refusing to march to the beat of someone else's drum

Insult

A behavior (verbal or otherwise) that conveys disrespect or contempt

A mean-spirited call out

Integrity

A well-developed sense of one's wholeness and sincerity

A marked degree of correspondence between one's actions and one's beliefs

Intellectual

One who lays claim to a superior intellect and expert opinions about all manner of subjects

One who intellectualizes (eschews feelings and emotions in favor of reasoned behavior and rational argument)

An Uncommon Vocabulary (4th Edition Revised)

Intelligence

The ability to accurately comprehend, to the degree possible, the confluence of circumstances (the tide of events)

A state of mental acuity that properly connects causes with effects and effects with causes, and that uses advantageously known connections between causes and effects

The right perception of pertinent influences

Intelligent

Memoried – *See also Knowledgeable*

Tenaciously experimental

Open-minded

Intention

A preliminary design – *See also Plan*

Intentional Harm

The injury that meanness originates and vengeful actions contemplated or taken perpetuate

Intolerant

Unwilling to give the benefit of the doubt to offending circumstances – *See also Reformer*

Intrusion

An incursion that is a precursor to an invasion

Intuition

A valid feeling without logic to go with it

Invincible

Apparently powerful to the point of being irresistible, but always with hidden weaknesses that can be exploited – *See also Chinks in the Armor*

Irksomeness of Change

The price one pays to overcome one's inertia

Irrationality

Logically explaining the unknowable
A state of mind that disdains reason – *See also Darkly Recalcitrant*

Irregularities

Those out-of-the-ordinary events in life that keep it from being a totally constrained and boring experience – *See also Regularities*

Irrelevant

Not able to directly affect one's present circumstances

J

Jerk

A malevolent manipulator

Joke

The brief amusing story that one is

Joy

A delightful emotion that attracts others to one's message and lends grace to one's actions

Joyful

Exhibiting joy for one's joy

> If all the griefs I am to have
> Would only come today.
> I am so happy I believe
> They'd laugh and run away.
> *Emily Dickinson*

Judge

To form an opinion based upon limited information

Judge Rightly

To reluctantly disparage the poor for their poverty, the oppressed for their oppression and the defeated for their defeats

To skeptically consider the fortunate wise and the unfortunate foolish

Justice

A doctrine of fairness that the powerful take pains to distort in their favor — *See also Victimize*

The ability to recompense injury with appropriate injury — *See also Revenge*

K

Karmic Justice
What goes around comes around

Keep It Simple
To prefer simplicity to complexity whenever and wherever complexity has no advantage over simplicity

Keep One's Distance
To maintain a psychological or physical space in which one is able to maneuver and yet still influence others – *See also Sphere of Influence*

Kid at Heart
One who maintains a high level of enthusiasm for life despite the ill effects of one's aging
One who fights maturity in good-natured ways

Kid Gloves
Gloves that allow one to damage one's opponent appropriately without leaving marks – *See also Friendly Game*

Kindness
A scattering of joy – *See also Attractiveness*
A gentle beautifier of complexion, form and behavior

Kindness to the Unkind
An encouragement for more unkindness

Kindred Spirit
One who understands that every living thing must struggle mightily to exist, and one who has a deep sympathy for these struggles

One who likes other people, and likes other living things

Knockdown
An overwhelming blow to one's person

A good reason to pick one's self up – *See also Defeat*

Knot
An annoying circumstance that requires careful unraveling or alternatively a decisive cutting through

Know
To understand enough to temporarily subdue one's doubt

Knowledge
Theoretical and practical understandings – *See also Comprehend*

Knowledgeable
Demonstrating the ability to recall relevant information

Demonstrating the ability to admit to a lack of knowledge if one is indeed ignorant of the matter

Known Universe
The markedly insufficient understanding of reality that human beings can somewhat agree upon

An Uncommon Vocabulary (4th Edition Revised)

A defective product of the human effort to understand the universe
IVS (Information Vetted Skeptically) and WAG (Wild-Ass
   Guesses) based upon IVS

L

Language

Associated (linked together) words – *See also Word*

The flawed human enterprise that attempts to convey information about and impart meaning to the changing, ambiguous, irregular, diverse, haphazard and misleading circumstances of life

Last Straw

A tipping-point event – *See also Tipping Point*

Lasting Agreement

The result of a just settlement

An agreement that both sides can live with – *See also Fair Price*

Laughter

Cheap medicine

An instant vacation

Law of Attraction

The hypothesis that one attracts into one's life what one thinks about consciously or unconsciously

The hypothesis that thoughts become things automatically

Leader

One whose direction is worth following

One who knows and knows that he knows, and who is capable of motivating others with this knowledge

Learn

To seek truth and find knowledge

Leave It and Move On

To abandon the irrelevant – *See also Irrelevant*

Legitimate Suffering

To suffer when necessary without being afraid of one's suffering
– *See also Neurosis*

Leisure Time

Downtime that provides one with the opportunity to appreciate
the mundane

Leniency

An appropriately tolerant reaction

Lesser Self

A less principled self – *See also Principled*
A self that demonstrates a weak commitment to right belief and
action – *See also Dishonor*

Lesson

The learning that occurs when life stoops to teach
A remembered experience that can be used to guide future
behavior – *See also Wise Up*

Let Bygones Be Bygones

To give up one's desire for revenge

Let Sleeping Dogs Lie
To stop dredging up the past

Liberal
One who believes that traditional ways of thinking and acting are open to scrutiny and change, and are not sacrosanct
A modernist

Lie
An untruth that makes doubtful all the truth that preceded it and all the truth that follows it
An unsustainable tale

Life
A journey with an unknowable destination – *See also Exist*
A trial by combat (biological, psychological and sociological warfare)
A farce-filled, capricious experience – *See also Reality*
A zero-sum effort

Life (2)
A manifestation of the innate capacities of the universe to replicate itself and to adorn itself with complexity

Life-Cycle of an Effort
Engage – Exert – Disengage – Recover

Life's Guarantees

No guarantees
No refunds
No exchanges

Limit

A behavioral or conditional boundary between the acceptable and
the unacceptable or the possible and the not possible that one
transgresses at one's peril – *See also Breakdown*

Listen

To distill meaningful sounds from background noise

Live

To make the best of the captivity that one is born into
To bloom where one is planted

Live and Let Live

To know the things one knows, to do the things one does and to
leave others to their own devices

Live in the Present

To consciously embrace who one is, what one is and where one is
To make now all that exists
To be concerned with the way things are, without regret for the
past or anxiety about the future
To eagerly take promptings from reality

The past is a smoking wick,
And the future a carrot on a stick.
Make now all that exists.
The present is as good as it gets.

Live with Contradictions

To occupy the tense space between opposing ideas – *See also Cognitive Dissonance*

Betwixt and between

Liveliness

The capacity to hold one's own against lifelessness – *See also Kid at Heart*

Living

An act of courage of the quiet sort

Logic

The capacity to reach apparently reliable conclusions based upon simplified explanations of complex phenomena – *See also Fact*

Logical Conclusion

A fundamentally inconclusive result that is a product of one's innately deficient logical reasoning

Loser's Attitude

Having lost today, the belief that one cannot win tomorrow

Losing Proposition
An endeavor that does not promise benefits that are sufficient to
justify the endeavor
A fool's errand
Actionable stupidity

Loss Limit
The point at which one will stop investing in a lost cause

Lost in the Trees
One who is unable to comprehend the forest for the trees
Overwhelmed by details – *See also Picky*

Love
Compelling affections for one's self and/or others
A pleasing reaction to being loved

Luck
The tide of events that one tends to attribute to merit if it is favorable and to randomness if it is unfavorable – *See also Fortune*

Lucky
Exhibiting the ability to prevail over the unfavorable odds that are
inherent in a situation

M

Madness
Senseless folly

Make a Smooth Transition
To maintain a proper swiftness of action that neither transforms
the purpose of the action with hurry, nor diminishes the purpose of the action with delay

Maladjusted
Prone to being frustrated, aggravated and shuffled off
Not willing to embrace one's nature

Malarkey
Hogwash – *See also Con*

Man's Rightful Dominion over Nature
The ludicrous idea that man has the capacity and the right to
control nature in some lasting way

Manage
To manipulate circumstances so that they have less of a chance to
derail a desired outcome
To grapple with realities

Manage Money

To make more money

To spend less money

To pitch one's scale of living some degrees below one's means

Martyr

One who willingly dies for an idea (a high price to pay for conjecture)

Masochist

One who derives pleasure from willfully hurting oneself – *See also Self-Harming*

Math

An abstract frame of reference for working out implications (a frame of reference that is not there until one puts it there) – *See also Do the Math*

Mature

To grow up

To be aware of the ambiguity of one's highest achievements (as well as one's deepest failures)

To become who one really is

Maudlin Mind

A mind overly affected with exaggerated feelings and misunderstood significances – *See also Bleeding Heart*

Meander

To wander in a state of pleasant distraction

Meaning

The significance of an event or thing as measured by the strength of one's feelings about it

Meaning-of-Life

The feelings of joy and sadness that ensue from the experience of living

Being born into a losing struggle with the will to fight the good fight

Measured Response

A remedy that is in proper proportion to the malady being remedied

Mental Anguish

Suffering based upon conjecture

Merit

The admirable qualities that abide when unworthiness is obvious
The worthiness that cloaks one's unworthiness

Mess Maker

The one who knows best how to clean up the mess, but the one least inclined to do so – *See also Responsibleness*

Metamorphosis
An attempted transformation of self that inevitably results in self-acceptance

Methodical
Exhibiting the ability to do the right things in the right order – *See also Procedure*

Mettle
One's toughness

Mind
Where one's thoughts come together and get sorted out
The sum total of one's mental faculties

Minimize
To inappropriately discount value, importance or difficulty

Miracle
A favorable event that could not be reasonably predicted
An event that encourages one to believe in the unpredictable

Misbehave
To act in unreasonable ways when it is self-serving to do so – *See also Behave*

Mistake
An erroneous judgment or action that is rarely fatal and frequently beneficial

Mitigate

To minimize the disadvantageous aspects of a disadvantageous situation

Mixed Bag

A self-professed saint and a skulking scoundrel compartmentalized in the same human being

Moderate

One who is inclined to reject the extremes of thought and action
A careful adopter of new ideas

Moderation

Nothing in excess
A commitment to sufficiency (just enough)

Mojo

The outward expression of one's self-confidence
One's swagger

Momentum

The tide of events that one must attempt to stem if it is unfavorable, or attempt to ride if it is favorable – *See also Wave*

Monkey on One's Back

A persistent desire that demands one's attention and depletes one's resources

Moral Judgment

An opinion held by one attempting to claim the high moral ground – *See also Self-Righteousness*

Morning Sun

The best light – *See also Rise and Shine*

Mortal Wound

An injury without remedy

Motion

A remedy for boredom and ennui

Motivated

Under the influence of one's motives – *See also Types of Motivation*

Motive

The reason for doing something that routinely eludes understanding

Move On

To abandon what one needs to abandon

To give up trying to settle a score

To get over it

To forget an injury by trusting that one will recall it without constant reminders

Muddle Through

To press on in a disorganized way towards a favorable outcome when one's distraction does not respect one's reason – *See also Distracted*

> Bits and pieces flirt with my troubled mind.
> Where lasting thoughts I seek to bind,
> Only vague, ghostly fragments are there to find.

Mull Over

To consider carefully the advantages and disadvantages inherent in an action

Misogynist

One who mistakenly believes that the female of the species is inferior to the male of species in all of the particulars that matter A chauvinist

Mystery

The circumstance that arouses one's curiosity, because it is extraordinary

Mystify

To intentionally create a mystery

N

Navigate
To pilot one's ship – *See also Ship*

Near Side
That which one focuses upon when the far side is too discouraging – *See also Far Side*
The shorter view

Necessary
That which remains when one eliminates the unnecessary – *See also Simplify*

Need
A personal necessity that one embraces and pursues in one's own way

Negative
Pessimistic
A counterproductive state of mind
A can't-do or won't-do attitude

Neurosis
A substitute for legitimate suffering
A dysfunctional expression of anxiety

New Day
A fresh start

Niche

A situation especially well-suited to one's interests, abilities and nature – *See also One's Path*

A comfortable rut

Nihilist

One who believes that the universe has no intrinsic meaning, other than the meanings that are ascribed to it by sentient (feeling) life forms that are bound up in its meaninglessness

No Action

One's inaction that can be superior to a bad action, and inferior to a good action

No-Nonsense Person

One who attends too much to the practical side of life to the detriment of a more imaginative existence

Noble Pretensions of Ignoble Persons

Feigned noble sentiments that provide the ignoble an opportunity to employ covertly their dastardly means – *See also Con (2)*

Nonconformist

One who is extremely honest and transparent

One who says what he thinks and does what he wants

One who refuses to fawn, flatter or pander

A loose cannon

An Uncommon Vocabulary (4th Edition Revised)

Nonsense

Thinking that is unhindered by reality

Nostalgia

A bittersweet longing for happiness past
A fond remembrance
The scent that survives the rose

> The fairest things have fleetest end,
> Their scent survives their close;
> But the rose's scent is bitterness
> to him that loved the rose
> *Francis Thompson*

Not-a-Penny

A penny saved at the expense of quality

Not-To-Do List

A daily list of activities not to engage in and thoughts not to entertain

Nothing

No things

Nothingness

Nonexistence
The lightless void
What one finds at the heart of things – *See also Heart of Things*

Numero Uno

The odd fellow at the top

O

Obedience

Feigned deference
Bowing to authority – *See also Sag*
Bending a knee

Obligation

An ongoing commitment that one endeavors to relieve oneself of

Obsession

A condition characterized by fixed and circular thoughts and
actions

Obstructionist

One who believes in obstinacy for the sake of obstinacy
One who is irrationally stubborn – *See also Hard Head*

Obvious

A readily apparent reality – *See also Unobvious*
A superficial aspect of reality (i.e. a solid, an absolute continuum,
a surface, a straight line, etc.)

Obvious Defense

The easiest defense to breach – *See also Stealth*

Off-Balance Opponent

A surprised opponent
A weaker adversary – *See also Harass*

Offense

An insult to one's self-importance

On the Edge of Chaos

A situation in which loss is imminent and safety non-existent
A set of circumstances that invigorates or paralyzes

> Heaven is not where the angles are
> Content and impervious to loss,
> But rather where the heart is,
> Ever on the edge of chaos.

On Time

In time most of the time

One's Book

The beliefs and attitudes that one has mentally chronicled as true

One's Life

A personal and personalized experience

One's Path

The path that no other person can travel – *See also Find One's Way*
Who one is

One's Purpose in Life

Any purpose that one subscribes to

One's Worth

The pleasing or displeasing subjective assessment of one's life-condition that takes into account the sum total of one's advantages discounted by the sum total of one's disadvantages

A personal opinion about one's value that one must actively protect from the whims and vagaries of circumstances — *See also Self-Respect*

One-Sided Relationship

A no-sided relationship in the making

Jack and Jill went up the hill
To fetch a pail of water
Jack came down
But Jill stuck around
To look for someone better

Open Book

A life-event that is open to examination and rumination

Open-Mindedness

The ability to understand more by understanding less
A state of mind that is open to wonder
A state of mind that is not closed by belief

Operative Words

The words and phrases that one uses to shape one's behavior

Opinionated Unnecessarily
Wasting precious thought and sentiment on the irrelevant – *See also Maudlin Mind*

Opportunism
Using advantageous circumstances selfishly – *See also Win*

Opportunity Cost
A reckoning of the missed opportunities that result from an ill-founded thought or action

Optimism
A favorable perspective on events that keeps the bounce in one's step and the sparkle in one's eye

Optimist
One who has confidence that there will be a favorable outcome – *See also Pessimist*
One who believes that what can go right will go right
One who sees the rose and not the thorns
A personification of spring

Optimistic
Imbued with optimism – *See also Positive*

Option-in-One's-Pocket
A plan of action that is kept to oneself

Order

The patterns that occur randomly in the midst of chaos

Orderliness

That which, when prolific enough, camouflages chaos

Organism

A viable (life-sustaining) complexity – *See also Complexity*
A living thing

Out-Spoken

One who speaks one's mind more or less clearly

Overachiever

One who tries too hard to do too much
One who aspires to be supernatural – *See also Aspire to be Supernatural*

Overcommit

To make a promise that one cannot keep – *See also Promise*

Overkill

The act of trying to win yet another battle when the war is won

Overreact

To take one's circumstances so seriously that one fails to note that they are not really serious

P

Pace Oneself
To compensate for fatigue by managing one's efforts

Pain
The messenger of injury – *See also Sore Wound*
Effort's bad side
A wakeup call
A hellish feeling

Panic
To paralyze oneself with one's own imaginings

Pantheist
One who believes that the universe is worthy of worship, because it is big, powerful and works in mysterious ways

Paralysis
The loss of the ability to function in the face of a frightening situation perceived as immutable

Pardon
To stay with pity the hand that would punish – *See also Leniency*

Passions
Personally preferred ways of making oneself happy
One's propellers

Past
That which has departed one's sphere of influence – *See also Sphere of Influence*
Smoking wicks
The dead, but not necessarily the buried

Path to Redemption
Being rightly ashamed of a wrongful deed – *See also Exonerate*

Patience
An even-temper that suppresses restlessness or annoyance
Timidity called by another name
A succor for anxiety, fear, discouragement and failure

Pay the Piper
To endure the unfavorable consequences of a pleasurable indiscretion – *See also Indiscretion*

Peace of Mind
A state of mind where one's circumstances do not warrant particular attention or indulgence
Having no opinion at all

Pencil
The best planning instrument

Perfection
Minimized imperfection

Perfectionist

One who cannot tolerate imperfection

Persist

To pursue a goal despite significant obstacles

To confirm through one's actions that one does not know when to give up

Persistent Dissatisfaction

A reliable source of unhappiness

The internal trappings of a futile hope

Personal Narrative

The ongoing conversation that one has with oneself – *See also Saying One's Say*

One's descriptions and prescriptions

One's feelings and emotions vocalized (expressed in words)

Self-talk

Personal Taboos

Personally imposed prohibitions against openly and honestly exploring one's desires, abilities and nature

Blockages of one's natural inclinations

Personality

The sum total of one's biological, psychological and sociological characteristics

The type of animal one is – *See also Kindred Spirit*

Perspective
A point of view arrived at by stepping back from a situation to get a better look

Pessimism
An unfavorable perspective on events that slows one's step and takes the sparkle from one's eye

Pessimist
One who does not have confidence in a favorable outcome
One who believes that what can go wrong will go wrong
One who sees the thorns and not the rose

Pessimistic
Imbued with pessimism – *See also Negative*

Petted and Pampered
Coddled to the point of not appropriately appreciating life's harshness

Philosopher
A thinker by trade
One who follows one's intellect to whatever conclusions it may lead

Physician
A healer of self
A healer of others

An Uncommon Vocabulary (4th Edition Revised)

Pickle

Between a rock and a hard place
On the horns of a dilemma
The main course of life

Picky

Excessively mired in the explicit details of life to the detriment of
a more serene and holistic existence

Pitiful Offense

An offense ineptly given

Pivot

To rapidly change the direction of one's thinking and/or actions

Plan

To figure out how to finish what one intends to start

Plan Less

To do more

Planet Earth

A speck of cosmic dust

Plans

Ideal configurations of future events that are fraught with all of
the shortcomings of idealism
Thought-out intentions

Jim Boyd

The best laid schemes o' mice an' men
Gang aft agley (Go oft awry).
An lea'e us nought
But grief and pain,
For promis'd joy!
Robert Burns

Play
To engage in an activity that relaxes or entertains — *See also Fun*

Play Dumb
To understand, but pretend that one does not

Play for Fun
To enjoy a game with no thought of serious or lasting consequences
Making the game the thing

Pleasure
The messenger of well-being
A heavenly feeling

Plug In
To incorporate an aspect of reality into one's thinking and actions
because it is conducive to one's well-being

Point
An advantage added to one's sum total of advantages — *See also Wealth*
A victory over a lesser self

Poison

A harmful concoction that often has a pleasing taste — *See also Aftertaste*

Positional Advantage

A position that compels one's opponent to struggle against unfavorable odds

The high ground

Positional Disadvantage

A position that surrenders the high ground to one's adversary

Positive

Optimistic

A productive state of mind

A can-do or will-do attitude

Possessed

Under the influence of a demon — *See also Demon*

Possible

Able to be done even when appearing undoable — *See also Impossible*

Pothole

A shallow rabbit hole — *See also Rabbit Hole*

Poverty

The sum total of the disadvantages that one must deal with

The sum total of the disadvantages that others must deal with

Power
A concentration of wealth, influence or physical strength that makes one prone to delusions of grandeur, entitlement and invincibility

A force to be reckoned with

Powerful
Exuding power

Practicality
Using what works and rejecting what does not work

Using what one has if what one has is sufficient

Prepare
To make ready for whomever and whatever, whenever

To equip oneself to take advantage of an opportunity – *See also Readiness*

Present
That which exists between the irrefutable past and the speculative future

The speechless real

One's circumstances that are as they are in part because they were as they were – *See also Past*

All that one ever has

Press On

To continue moving forward as if it were not optional – *See also Persist*

Pressure

A compelling or restraining force or influence that one internally generates, or that arises externally and then is internalized – *See also Safety Valve*

Coercion

Pretension

A fraudulent claim to quality or merit

Price

That which must be given, done, or undergone in order to reach a desired goal

A physical and mental toll exacted on one for acting or not acting (both action and inaction have costs associated with them)

Price Control

The act of shopping around – *See also Fair Price*

Not buying something simply because it is expensive

Pride

Making oneself the object of one's affections

Primal Fear

The fear of being annihilated (reduced to nothingness)

Principle

A rule derived from a belief

Principled

One who follows rules that are worth following – *See also Rule Worth Following*
One who is honorable

Proactive

Demonstrating the ability to act in the present to preempt or bring about a future event

Procedure

The simplest description of a process that is sufficient to produce a desired result
An efficient habit

Procrastinate

To save one's efforts when circumstances are able to resolve themselves
To put off that which can be done easier at a later time

Progress

Necessity called by another name
A measurable change for the better

Progressive

One who embraces and promotes change
A change agent

An early adopter of new ideas
A futurist

Promise

The assurance made to gain or retain the trust of another

Proof

Evidence that is sufficient to establish a hypothesis as true or false
Evidence that is sufficient to establish a hypothesis as partially true and partially false – *See also Hypothesis*

Punctual

Demonstrating the ability to adhere to a schedule

Purity

An impossible to attain state of oneness – *See also Distillate*

Purpose

An intended outcome
A prerequisite for enthusiasm

Pursue Excellence

To dedicate oneself to outdoing others or oneself

Pursue Happiness

To strive to increase one's joy or reduce one's sadness
To accumulate quality experiences

Push Back

A resistive response to being pushed

Put Up a Front

To mount a vigorous defense of appearances

Q

Quality Experience
An experience that confirms one's abilities to explore, engage and
enjoy life

Question
A mechanism for garnering knowledge
An expression of one's uncertainty
What, Why, When, How, Where and Who

> I KEEP six honest serving-men
> (They taught me all I knew);
> Their names are What and Why and When
> And How and Where and Who.
> *Rudyard Kipling*

Quiet Interval
The interval of time between the most recent ending and the next
beginning – *See also Respite*

Quitter
One who gives up prematurely
One who responds to adversity with helplessness

R

Rabbit Hole

An effort that promises to become stranger, more problematic, more difficult, more complex or more chaotic as one commits additional resources to the undertaking – *See also Pothole*

Radical Idea

An idea capable of effecting fundamental changes in one's attitudes and beliefs

An idea that is extraordinary

Radical Thinker

One who entertains radical ideas

One in tune with reality's radicalness

A freethinker

Rash Action

An action justified by anger or frustration that as a rule turns out badly when feelings cool and circumstances change – *See also Aggravate an Injury*

Rational Behavior

Evidence-based actions

Actions based upon necessarily superficial logical assumptions – *See also Logical Conclusion*

React

To do the obvious in response to the obvious
To act without thinking about possible consequences

Readiness

The ability to do what one needs to do when one needs to do it

Realist

One who sees the rose discounted by the thorns
One who sees the thorns discounted by the rose
One who believes that reality can be perceived in some definite
    and final way

Reality

The half-truths that one must generally accept as the whole truth
    in order to enjoy some semblance of happiness
Those aspects of one's existence that one dearly embraces as real
That which one proves to oneself exists
A collective hunch

Reality-As-It-Is

That which is never exactly what one says it is or computes that
    it is
The snowflake that is not a snowflake, that is not a snowflake (ad
    infinitum)
2 snowflakes that are not 2 snowflakes, that are not 2 snowflakes
    (ad infinitum)

Really?

An expression of wonderment that is particularly well-suited to preposterous assertions and ridiculous events

Reason

To imperfectly derive causes from effects
To imperfectly predict effects from causes

Reasonable

Constrained by reason – *See also Sensible Person*
One who listens to the voice of reason

Reasonable Probability

The only certainty

Reassurance

A comforting feeling that accompanies finding an approximation of the old in the new

Rebel

To not do that which one has been trained to do
To break the mold

Reborn

Revived and rejuvenated by an idea

Recipe for Weight Loss

Move more and eat less

Reciprocity

Responding to kindness with kindness and to hurt with hurt – *See also Justice*

Reckless Plan

A plan born of desperation and evincing foolhardiness – *See also Grasping at Straws*

Reconcile

To reach a just settlement
To bury the hatchet

Recover

To move beyond one's pain

Reductionist

One who mistakenly believes that there is something in the universe that is whole and of one piece – *See also God Particle*

Reductionist Process

The reductionist's attempt to produce something that is irreducible – *See also Purity*

Reform

To change the rules of a game to one's advantage

Reformer

One who refuses to tolerate offending circumstances

Refuse to Imagine
To stop imagining

Regret
To be unable to enjoy one's present circumstances because of lingering guilt – *See also Wallow*

Regularities
The repetitive aspects of life that keep it from being a totally absurd and preposterous experience – *See also Irregularities*

Relax
To coast for a while – *See also Coast to the Line*
To stop resisting

Relax fully and well.
For who can really tell?
Without resistance to keep them tight,
One's restraints may slip away without a fight.

Relevant
Able to affect one's present circumstances

Remarkable
Something that is worth making remarks about

Remedy
To repair what is broken
To make an annoyance go away

Remedy Boredom

To amuse oneself

Remedy Loneliness

To more freely converse with the not-you

Remembrance

A mental souvenir

Reminder

That which spurs one to remember what is dead and buried

Remorse

A personal reckoning
The usually too severe judgment of one's past actions

Remorseful

Deeply sorry

Residue

That which remains after the dust settles – *See also Dust*

Resilient

Adept at bouncing back – *See also Comeback*
Able to take a licking and keep on ticking – *See also Mettle*

Resolution

A promise made to oneself

Resolve

To commit to a course of action
To make a promise to oneself

Respite

A beneficial period of rest taken between exertions – *See also Quiet Interval*
A slow down zone

Responsibleness

Calmly owning whatever comes along, bubbles up or spills out
Cleaning up a mess, one's own or that of another

Rest

To recover from one's exertions – *See also Life-Cycle of an Effort*
To refuse to be further seduced by the undone

Result

An outcome of an experiment that one can use to one's advantage in the next experiment
An answer provided by the general order of things

Resurrect

To dig up the dead and buried

Return to Sender

To send a disagreeableness back to its source with vigor – *See also Reciprocity*

Revenge

Retaliation for a recent or long-remembered wrong – *See also Justice*

Payback

Reverse Psychology

The practice of disparaging one's own capacities and plans, so that one's natural contrariness can rise to the occasion to prove the assertions wrong

Revolution

What goes up on the backs of men comes down by the hands of men

Revolving-Door Universe

A universe that ceaselessly traffics in comings and goings
A universe that practices recycling on a grand scale

Rhetoric

Empty talk
Expressing small ideas with many words

Ridiculousness

Actions, thoughts or beliefs that are worthy of ridicule (withering criticism)

Right

Proven correct in action, judgment, opinion or method

Right (2)

The inalienable capacity to do or not to do whatever the confluence of circumstances permits

Right Action

An action that one is personally comfortable with
An action that feels right

Right Answer

The answer that relieves the tension of the question

Right Question

The question that goes to the heart of the matter for an answer –
See also Heart of the Problem

Righteousness

Pompous goodness
A mask for wickedness

Rise and Shine

To wake up by getting up
To get moving

> O! it's nice to get up in the mornin'
> when the sun begins to shine,
> At four or five or six o'clock
> in the good old summer time
> When the snow is snowin'

and its murky over head
O! it's nice to get up in the mornin',
but it's nicer to lie in bed
Traditional Scottish Song

Rise to the Occasion
To demonstrate skill and/or courage in response to a difficult or
dangerous situation

Risky Business
An activity that requires one to take chances

Rock Bottom
A markedly dysfunctional mental and physical state that motivates one to finally disavow the completely useless behaviors
that got one there – *See also Comeback*

Rule
A principle that governs one's conduct that one chooses to believe
is personally beneficial
A precept that often requires bending
A line in the sand – *See also Draw a Line in the Sand*

Rule Worth Following
A rule that makes life a more worthwhile experience, not by edict
but in fact

Ruminate

To continuously think about that which one does not sufficiently understand – *See also Turn Every Which Way but Loose*

Rumor

A report that is typically short on facts and rife with speculations

S

Sadist

One who happily contributes to the furtherance of human suffering with no regard for the fact that suffering abounds in the human condition – *See also Jerk*

Sadness

A fatigued enthusiasm for life

Safety

A secure and settled state of mind and body that no station in life supports

That which one paradoxically finds in growth, reform and change

Safety Valve

A behavior the sole purpose of which is to depressurize (to let off steam) – *See also Pressure*

Sag

To appropriately droop under the weight of the world – *See also Bend*

Sanity

The ability to behave normally

Minimized abnormality – *See also Insanity*

Saying One's Say

To express forthrightly in words one's ideas, values and beliefs

To speak one's mind

Scar

Evidence of healing

Scheme

To actively plot against failure

Science

Methodical truth seeking

Scientific Method

Observe an aspect of the universe

Create a hypothesis (a tentative description) of this aspect

Make predictions based upon the hypothesis

Test these predictions with experiments or further observations

Determine if the results of the experiments or observations are consistent with the predictions

If the results are not consistent with the predictions, do it all again

If the results are consistent with the predictions, chronicle the hypothesis as true – *See also One's Book*

Score

To improve one's circumstances and oneself – *See also Elevate One's Game*

Scratch Where It Itches

To do as one pleases

Secret to a Long Life

One's genetic material that is conducive to longevity

An Uncommon Vocabulary (4th Edition Revised)

Self
The totality of one's circumstances

Self Forgive
To reach a level of understanding or compassion for oneself that quells one's self-blaming

Self-Acceptance
The ability to embrace as equals one's strengths and one's defects so that one or the other cannot claim the high ground of one's regard

Accepting oneself as one is

Considering oneself sufficient and not in need of further improvement

Self-Assertion
Claiming a place in the general order of things

Being the hammer and not the anvil

Self-Compassion
Willing to help oneself, because one needs the help

Expressing sympathy and kindness for oneself

An intentional softening of one's negative self-judgments by acknowledging that one is mortal, vulnerable and imperfect

Self-Confidence
One's arrogance tempered by experience

Full trust in the effectiveness of one's habits of thought and action

Living with a steady superiority over life

Self-Control
Quibbling with oneself about large and small matters

Self-Deception
A devious game governed by unobvious rules that one plays with oneself
Telling oneself a cleverly rendered lie

Self-Defeating
Exhibiting the capacity to be one's own worst enemy – *See also Self-Inflicted Wound*

Self-Defense
Protecting oneself from all types of harm – *See also Self-Preservation*

Self-Deprivation
The practice of restraining oneself for restraint's sake – *See also Personal Taboos*

Self-Doubt
Lacking confidence in one's habits of thought and action
A saving grace for those afflicted with arrogance
Doubting one's first principles
Suspecting that a core belief is not true – *See also Core Belief*

Self-Expression
To externally display one's internal disposition

Self-Forgiveness

An appropriate pardoning of oneself when one has suffered enough or when one is suffering sufficiently without the added burden of self-reproach

Self-Harming

Making oneself the object of one's disaffection
Incurring harm by acting without due regard for one's well-being

Self-Image

A condensed and over-simplified rendering of oneself to oneself

Self-Improvement

To weaken one's vices by neglecting to indulge them
To strengthen one's virtues by intentionally exercising them

Self-Inflicted Wound

A personally gratifying injury that is intentionally incurred – *See also Masochist*
The most difficult wound to heal

Self-Interest

The selfishness that abides where there is altruism

Self-Loathing

One's denigration of oneself to oneself to the detriment of a more prideful and exemplary existence

Self-Made

Having achieved a level of success or recognition, to disdain all
supportive relationships and confluent circumstances, even to
the point of denying normal birthing

Self-Pity

Personal sorrow for the real or imagined injustices than one must
endure
An excuse to wallow in the face of adversity – *See also Ineffectualness*

Self-Pity, self-pity, what say thee?
"Poor me, poor me, saddened unjustly."
But where is the justice that I seek?
Is it only for the strong and not the weak?

Self-Preservation

The act of saving one's self if one is in need of saving

Self-Reproach

Criticizing oneself for good reason
The elevation of one's defects over one's strengths in one's regard
Self-blaming

Self-Respect

Duly impressed with oneself
The elevation of one's strengths over one's defects in one's regard

Self-Righteousness

A pious attitude – *See also Righteousness*
Noting the faults of others to the exclusion of one's own

There is so much good in the worst of us
And so much bad in the best of us
That it hardly behooves any of us
To talk about the rest of us.
Edward Wallis Hoch

Self-Sacrifice

The forfeiting of one's present happiness in order to pursue one's future happiness – *See also Foolish Thrift*

Self-Serving Deception

A preferred maneuver of a game player

Selfishness

The honest and direct expression of one's interests and desires
Attending to one's needs – *See also Need*

Semantics

Shady meanings

Sense

To rawly perceive without verbally interpreting – *See also Reality-As-It-Is*
To see what one sees – *See also Eyes Wide Open*

Sense of Loss

The sadness that accompanies the severing of a valued bond – *See also Bond*

Sensible Person

One who is slow to abandon reason for the sake of nonsense – *See also Reasonable*

Sensibility

One's taste for what is good and proper in a given situation

Sensitivity

The condition of being appropriately or excessively affected by internal or external stimuli

Share the Load

To allow others to help – *See also Ask for Help*

Shine

To occupy center stage and to prevail marvelously – *See also Center Stage*

Shining Example

A best in class
Oneself (in a league of one's own) – *See also Uniqueness*

Ship

An imaginary floating repository of one's happiness that may never see port – *See also Navigate*

Shoulda, Woulda, Coulda

A proper send-off for pestering guilt

Shtick

A theatrical routine that one employs to entertain or seduce others

A behavioral gimmick used by those who need to be the center of attention

Sickness

Biological warfare

The harbinger of non-being

Silence

Appropriate quietness when sound does not help

Simple Answer

An answer that defies the complexity of the question

Simple Pleasure

A pleasure easily found and easily enjoyed – *See also Take One's Pleasure*

Simple Question

A question asked to elicit a simple answer

A question that often elicits a complex answer where a simple answer is anticipated

Simplify

To eliminate the unnecessary so that one can attend to the necessary

To strip reality of its nuances (subtleties)

Sitting in the Catbird Seat

Sitting pretty – *See also Easy Street*

Occupying that rare perch that allows one to feel superior to circumstances

Skepticism

A healthy disrespect for easy answers

Not taking a person, a thing, an idea, a doctrine or a situation at face value

A firm discounting of extravagant claims of worth and worthlessness

Slack

A level of tolerance that one affords to an irritating person or situation

Sleep

The state of unawareness that precedes waking

The quiet healer of life's ills that employs comforting natural remedies that the waking body has no time to use

Slippery Slope

An idea or action that can lead directly to a tipping-point event – *See also Tipping Point*

Slow Play

To act weak when one is strong – *See also Bluff*

Small Stuff

That which when gathered together becomes big stuff
Everything

Smart Move

A favorable action that is always a mix of intelligence and dumb luck

Snap Decision

An expeditious decision occasioned by demanding circumstances
The most prevalent type of decision

Social Grievance

An injury that warrants addressing in the social context in which it arises

Soft-Spoken

One who speaks quietly and with gentle intentions – *See also Suggestion*

Solve a Mystery

To provide an ordinary explanation for an extraordinary event

Sore Wound

An injury in need of immediate remedy

Sorrow

The condition of being sad about one's sadness

Soul

The vitality (replicative energy) that permeates and animates a living thing

The will-to-live that dissipates with death, and that is fully reconstituted at birth — *See also Birth*

Sound

Appropriate clamor when silence does not help — *See also Silence*

Sound Purpose

A purpose worth pursuing — *See also Winning Proposition*

Spark

The energetic effect that results from striking opportunistically — *See also Opportunism*

Speculate

To read more into something than there is in it to be read

Speechless Real

Reality as it is — *See also Reality-As-It-Is*

Spell

A strong compelling attraction or influence — *See also Break a Spell*

Sphere of Influence

The extent to which one can effectively affect others

The extent to which events are responsive to one's actions

Spirited

Alive

Spiritual

To be in awe of the majesty and mystery of it all

Spontaneous

Letting a single impulsive thought be enough to justify an action
    – *See also Snap Decision*

Staged Breathing

One breath in - One breath out – One breath in – One breath out
    (repeated until one's composure returns)

Staging

To put the necessary pieces in place before one acts – *See also
    Facilitate*

Stamina

The strength to tenaciously move on – *See also Mettle*

Stand Down

To stop being a hero

Stand Up

To refuse to kneel before the world as if it is an idol worthy of
    worship
To fight for something that one believes in

Do you fear the force of the wind,
The slash of the rain?
Go face them and fight them,
Be savage again.
Go hungry and cold like the wolf,
Go wade like a crane.
The palms of your hands will thicken,
The skin of your cheek will tan,
You'll grow ragged and weary and swarthy,
But you'll walk like a man!
Hamlin Garland

Star Gaze

To focus upon the far, far away to the detriment of what is near at hand

Starting Place

Where one is

Stay

To not run away
To demonstrate strength in the midst of weakness

Stay Loose

To remain calm and capable by being opportunistic (using advantageous circumstances selfishly), and not by being egotistic (believing that one can manipulate circumstances to one's advantage)

Stay the Course

To proceed along one's current path with a stubbornness that yields only to necessity – *See also Press On*

Stealth

The act of removing sound and fury from the equation of action

Steer Away from Pain

To steer towards pleasure – *See also Pursue Happiness*

Step Up

To lead

Stillness

Calmness in response to noise and scurry

Stimulant

That which arouses or animates one to act

Stingy

Disinclined to be generous for fear that one's excessive wealth may become merely sufficient wealth

Stopping Place

A pose that one can hold

Straight Shooter

One who dismays tacticians by straightforwardly expressing his or her sentiment

One who uses common sense and practices plain dealing

Straight-Line Thinker

One who mistakenly believes that the shortest distance between two points in space and time is a straight line

Strain

Painful effort

Silent suffering

Stream of Consciousness

One's conscious reactions to internal or external events

Strength Train

To make life harder than it needs to be so that one becomes leaner and tougher

Stress-Coping Mechanisms

One's thoughts, words and actions

Stressor

Reality as one perceives it

Strings

One's sensitivities that are exploited by jerks

Stronger
Capable of better managing one's weaknesses

Struggle
To make one's way in life by contending resolutely with powerful adversaries and ever-present opposing forces

Studied Judgment
A carefully considered judgment that is particularly valuable when one is harried

Stupid Idea
An idea that encourages one to act stupidly

Stupid Utterance
A question asked or a remark made without forethought or discretion

Stupidity
Refusing to accurately comprehend, to the degree possible, the confluence of circumstances (the tide of events)

A diminished state of mental acuity that cannot properly connect causes with effects and effects with causes, or that denies known connections between causes and effects

The wrong perception of pertinent influences

Subordinate
One who marches to the beat of someone else's drum – *See also Duty*

Substitute

A less than satisfying alternative

Success

A plan of action that turns out well
A moving target
The thrill of victory – *See also Victory*

Succinct

Using one word if one word will do instead of two
Pithy

Sucker

One who is particularly gullible – *See also Gullible*
One who is vulnerable to sucker punches

Sucker Punch

A harmful blow that comes from a surprising quarter

Suffering

A painful physical condition that is routinely necessary for learning
Mental anguish
A requisite condition of life – *See also Bitched*

Suggestion

A gentle piece of advice

Suitable Vice

A tranquilizer for a troubled mind

An unsavory behavior that helps one steady one's ship

Superficial Remedy

A remedy that wastes time and effort by having no discernible effect on a problem – *See also Edges of a Problem*

Superior Course of Action

The course of action that will result in the least harm and the most good

Superiority Complex

Delusions of grandeur

Suppression

Discounting the importance or relevance of an incompatible idea, value or belief, so that it does not interfere with the ideas, values or beliefs that are currently impelling one's behavior

Surf

To successfully ride the crest of a wave of feeling – *See also Wave*

Surprise

An unexpected action that delights one's friends and/or aggravates one's enemies

Survive

To tenaciously occupy space and time with one's fragile form
To continue to exist by being adaptive and lucky – *See also Adapt*

Switch Gears

To increase or decrease the rapidity of one's thoughts or actions
To broaden or narrow one's perspective
To change one's approach

Sympathy

A feeling of sadness for the distress of another living thing – *See also Empathy*

Synergistic Personality

One who needs things to work out well selfishly (to meet one's needs) and, at the same time, unselfishly (to meet the needs of others)

One who possesses and expresses sets of opposing personality traits (i.e. tough and sensitive, proud and humble, selfish and unselfish, cooperative and rebellious, analytic and metaphoric, sympathetic and unsympathetic, shy and bold, etc.)

One who copes with changing circumstances by maintaining reversibility (the ability to respond in one way or its opposite in any situation)

T

Take a Chance

To expose oneself to danger or loss
To put oneself in the way of luck

Take It or Leave It Attitude

The disposition to do whatever one feels like doing or to not do
whatever one feels like not doing – *See also Right (2)*

Take One's Pleasure

To avail oneself of a pleasurable opportunity before it runs away
to hide as it is wont to do – *See also Indulge*

Take the Initiative

To overcome one's inertia

Talking Point

An aspect of one's life that one chooses to put into words

Talking To

A verbal chastising

Test

To determine the validity of an idea through the application of
it – *See also Experiment*

Tethered
Constrained by the perceived benefits of one's circumstances – *See also Cheese*

Thankful
Appreciating the advantages that one enjoys
Gratefully noting the disadvantages that one does not have to deal with

Theist
One who believes that universe was created and is governed by benevolent and malevolent personalities (In the case of the monotheist, a single personality gets all of the credit.)

Thing
An eddy in the confluence of circumstances

Think about the Weight
To double the load

Think Less
To do more

Think More
To do less – *See also Plan*

Thorns in One's Side
The prickers (male, female or otherwise) that one encounters as part of life

Thought

The mental process that uses abstractions to model a hodgepodge
of entities and nothingness
The music of the mind
One's stream of consciousness

Thrill Seeker

An adrenalin addict

How are you doing? Just fine.
Up and down all of the time.
No happy medium.
Excitement or tedium.

Tide of Events

The confluence (flowing together nature) of circumstances

Tidiness

A place for everything, and everything in its place

Tight Place

A place where smaller is better

Time

The drumbeat of existence that one marches to

Timidity

Unwarranted hesitancy – *See also Indecision*
Wimpiness – *See also Wimpy*

Jim Boyd

Tipping Point

A situation in which a small event added to the sum total of events can trigger significant and irreversible effects – *See also Last Straw*

To-Do List

A daily list of activities to engage in and thoughts to entertain

Token Effort

An appropriately weak effort when one is on the wrong track – *See also Wise Reserve*

Tolerate

To give the benefit of the doubt to offending circumstances

Tough

Resistant and resilient

Toxic Mix

Arrogance and ignorance

Toy

A thing that amuses

Tradition

A revered habit

Traditionalist
One who believes that traditions are sacrosanct, and not open to scrutiny or change

Trap
A contrivance for ensnaring and rendering one's adversary vulnerable to harm

Trash Talk
Verbal stupidity – *See also Zip It*
Free speech not worth listening to

> Nothing is so good for an ignorant man
> as silence
> and if he knew this,
> he would no longer be ignorant.
> *Sa'di*

Travel Light
To live unencumbered by baggage

Trick
A clever means to an end

Trickster
One who knows and uses many tricks

Trip Wire

An emotional string that when pulled has a considerable unpleasantness on the other end – *See also Unfortunate Jerk*

Troubles

One's afflictions sent packing with a knowing smile and a see-you-later wink

What's the use of worrying
It never was worthwhile
So pack up your troubles in your old kit bag
And smile, smile, smile
First World War Marching Song

True Colors

A display of the naked truth – *See also Acknowledgement*

Trust

Well-placed or misplaced confidence

Thrust ivrybody – but cut th' ca-aards.
Peter Finley Dunne

Truth

That which one finds after stripping away duplicity
An unforced agreement between the experience and the description of it
A vetted (verified) opinion

Turn Every Which Way but Loose

To tenaciously seek an answer – *See also Ruminate*

Tweak

A minor adjustment that promises to make a successful endeavor
more successful, or an unsuccessful endeavor successful

A small change that can make a big difference

Types of Insults

The insult that is given, but not taken

The insult that is not given, but taken

The insult that is given and taken

Types of Motivation

Doing something because one needs to

Doing something because one is supposed to

Doing something because one wants to

U

Ugliness
The quality of being repulsive to others by engendering unhappiness in them

Ulterior Motive
The motive behind a deception – *See also Crook*

Ultimate Question
Why is there something rather than nothing?
The question that is particularly vulnerable to absurd answers

Unaddressed Problem
The problem that will bite one in the ass the first chance that it gets

Unaffected
Without pretentions emanating from a perceived superiority to or a separateness from the universe – *See also Holistic Thought*

Unavoidable Danger
An imminent and pressing danger that it is best to welcome with clear intentions and aplomb – *See also Daring*

Uncertainty
That aspect of life that makes every action to some degree an experiment, and every projected outcome of these experiments a probability (a rigorous guess about the likelihood of an outcome being realized)

Underachiever
One who deprives oneself of success by trying too little – *See also Overachiever*

Underreact
To not take one's circumstances seriously enough to reach an understanding concerning them

Understand
To mentally grasp connections, correlations and contingencies

Undisciplined
Having no personal commitment to harmful or ineffective rules of conduct

Unenvious
One who is able to say the words, "I'd rather be me.", and mean them

Unfortunate
Having the bad luck to be in the wrong place at the wrong time without the abilities necessary to ameliorate the situation
Incurring harm from going in the wrong direction for the right reasons

Unfortunate Jerk
A jerk appropriately rewarded – *See also Trip Wire*

Ungrateful

Not appreciating the advantages that one enjoys

Not gratefully noting the disadvantages that one does not have to deal with

Unhappiness

Not having one's day

Not saying one's say

The aftertaste of a bad action – *See also Aftertaste*

The feeling state that accompanies an unsuccessful experiment

Unintended Destination

The unanticipated destination that arrives with its attendant point of view

Uniqueness

One's particular nature, circumstances and abilities that successfully defy the summary judgments of others – *See also Be Different*

Universal Constant

The ever-present instability of the universe – *See also Change*

Universe

An ignorant brute that is overly appreciated by some, who believe that they see method in its madness, and underestimated by others, who believe that they are somehow immune to its brutishness

A flawed environment that imperfectly rewards intelligence and imperfectly punishes stupidity

Jim Boyd

Ah, Love! could thou and I with Fate conspire
To grasp this sorry Scheme of Things entire!
Would not we shatter it to bits-and then
Re-mould it nearer to the Heart's Desire!
Omar Khayyám

Unknowable
The postulated reality lying behind all phenomena, but not know-
able by any of the processes by which the mind becomes con-
scious of phenomenal objects – *See also Elephant in the Room*
The reality that is excluded from one's perceptions of reality
The lion beyond the firelight

Touch a rose and feel it grow.
And realize that you will never know
From whence it came and to whither it will go.

Unlucky
Not able to benefit from the favorable odds that are inherent in
a situation

Unmotivated
Appropriately or inappropriately not inclined to use one's talents
or to exercise one's strengths
Motiveless – *See also Disinterestedness*

Unnecessaries
Those things that can be sacrificed for the sake of a simpler and
easier life – *See also Baggage*

Unobvious

That which abides despite the obvious – *See also Obvious*
Underlying realities that are not readily apparent
Reality's private face

Unplug

To exclude an aspect of reality from one's thinking and actions, because it is not conducive to one's well-being

Unreasonable

Not expecting to incur the logically projected consequences of one's actions
Not constrained by reason

Unreasonableness

The act of abandoning reasoned behaviors and beliefs when they are ineffective – *See also Darkly Recalcitrant*

Unstoppable Opponent

An opponent to hinder

Unwelcome Memory

An irritating remembrance – *See also Bad Memory*

Unworthiness

The undesirable qualities that abide when worthiness is obvious
The undesirable qualities that cloak one's worthiness

Upstream Problem
A problem that cannot be resolved with downstream solutions

Use Discretion
To tell not all one knows
To believe not all one hears
To do not all one is able

Utopian
One who believes that idealism can win out – *See also Idealism*
One who believes that there is stability to be found in this unstable universe – *See also Universal Constant*

V

Vacation
A change of pace that relaxes and/or entertains

Vain
Excessively impressed with oneself – *See also Superiority Complex*

Vainglory
One's glorification of oneself to oneself to the detriment of a humbler and more unassuming existence

Valuable Resource
The resource that one spends well

Verify
To seek out information that will minimize one's doubt

When in doubt,
Thrash about.
Beat the bushes for the truth.
Be an aggressive sleuth.

Vet
To rigorously verify

Vexation
A tenacious irritator

Vexed

Confounded (frustrated and confused) by a vexation – *See also Demon*

Vice

A harmful habit

A habit that can run away inappropriately with one's time and resources – *See also Monkey on One's Back*

A rebellion against virtue

Victimize

To harm others under the guise of being just

Victory

A temporary subjugation of one's opposition and not the final word on anything

Vigorous

Inclined to and capable of testing one's limits and the limits of others

Violence

A meeting of force with force resulting in woe for the weaker

Virtue

A beneficial habit

A rebellion against vice

A habit that can make good use of one's time and resources

Vocabulary

The words that are particular to and essential for one's understandings of circumstances – *See also Word*

W

Wake Up
To become conscious of one's circumstances

Waking
The state of awareness that precedes sleep – *See also Eyes Wide Open*

Walk the Talk
To practice what one preaches – *See also Hypocrite*

Wallow
To perversely enjoy one's misery – *See also Self-Pity*

War
A bitter struggle between opposing points of view that when won quietly, minimizes collateral damage

Warning
A cautionary tale that benefits only those who will listen

Wave
A surge of effects
The standard manner in which influences arrive

Weak Excuse
The excuse that needs an excuse
The excuse that is inferior to not making an excuse

Jim Boyd

Weakness
A state of diminished capacities and sensibilities
A poor substitute for strength
Weariness

Wealth
The sum total of the advantages that one enjoys

Weigh Options
To give equal time to opposing ideas — *See also Mull Over*

Well-Adjusted
Healthy, wealthy and wise
Willingly embracing one's nature

Whole
That which is not a thing, but contains all things

Why Not Here? Why Not Now?
A proper send-off for one's timidity — *See also Call Out*
Fighting words

Wild Hair
An urge to be unwise
A mad notion

Willfulness

Continuing to do what one wants to do
Continuing to say what one wants to say
Continuing to believe what one wants to believe

Willingness

Consenting to play one's part in a scheme that is not of one's own
   making
Going along to get along – *See also Conformist*

Willpower

Dedicating one's mental resources to the accomplishment of a difficult task – *See also Concentrate*

Wily

Exhibiting the capacity to determine what it is that other people
   want one to want, and then to decide if one really wants what
   they want

Wimpy

Holding to the premise that one is a milksop

Win

To achieve success through anticipation, preparation and opportunism

Win Goal

A goal that when met and adhered to allows one to step away a
   winner

Winner's Attitude

Having won today, the belief that one will win tomorrow – *See also Loser's Attitude*

Believing that one will win out

Winning Proposition

An endeavor that promises benefits that are sufficient to justify the endeavor

Actionable intelligence

Wisdom

Well-founded beliefs

Wise

Basing one's thoughts and actions upon well-founded beliefs

One who understands that foolishness is inescapable

One who knows and knows that he knows

Wise Guy

One who is successful in an unwise endeavor

Wise Reserve

A store of uncommitted resources that results from a reluctance to invest wholeheartedly in an endeavor when one's aims are unclear or one's means are lacking – *See also Token Effort*

Wise Up

To learn from experience – *See also Lesson*

The road to wisdom – Well it's plain
and simple to express:
Err
and err
and err again
but less
and less
and less.
Piet Hein

Wishful Thinking

Believing in the illusion that a hoped-for result can be realized by
simply wishing and hoping that it will come true – *See also*
Law of Attraction

Believing that the unknowable will someday be known

Believing that one can escape the mischief of one's vices and the
rewards of one's virtues

Believing that one's virtues can protect one from all types of harm

Believing that one's vices do not have redeeming qualities

Believing that virtue and vice are not blood brothers (albeit con-
tentious ones)

Wonder

A feeling of admiration for something that is perceived as
remarkable

Inquisitiveness

Word

An artifact of speech

A sound bite

A device for conveying information about and ascribing meanings to circumstances

Work

Labor exchanged for sustenance

The undesirable labors that the fortunate pass on to the less fortunate

Working Definition

A type of definition in which a new or currently existing word or phrase is given a personally useful meaning that may, but does not necessarily, differ from or contradict a dictionary (lexical) definition

A definition of a word or a phrase that facilitates one's thinking and actions within a given set of circumstances

A personally ascribed meaning of a word or phrase

Worse

Exhibiting a comparative disadvantage in the eye of the beholder that may actually be a comparative advantage if worse is on the way to better – *See also Better*

Worshiper

One who fawns, flatters and panders in hopes of gaining the favor of an authority figure

Worth of the Stimulation

The quality of the satisfaction

Wrong

Proven not correct in action, judgment, opinion or method

Wrong Action

An action that one is not personally comfortable with
An action that no amount of reasoning can make right
An action that feels wrong

Y

Yielding

A conciliatory practice that is evidence of one's weakness or error

Z

Zero-Sum Effort

An effort the benefits of which are equal to the resource expenditures needed to make the effort

An effort that produces zero net gain and zero net loss – *See also Life*

A wash

Zip It

To fortuitously stop talking to oneself and/or to others

To adopt an attitude of silence for the purpose of clarifying the elusive or revealing the deceptive

To stop trash talking – *See also Trash Talk*

Epilogue

Gaps and spaces are all right.
Just look at the starry night.
Without the endless darkness,
Could the stars shine as bright?
And when your logic is without a flaw
And you have found an eternal law,
Remember that a life without confusion
Is a grand illusion.
Perfection is stagnation,
And the universe will have none of it.